State of Vermont
Department of Libraries
Midstate Regional Library
RFD #4
Montpelier, Vt. 05602

WITHDRAWN

The Trumpet Book

The Trumpet Book

BY MELVIN BERGER

Illustrated with Photographs

Lothrop, Lee & Shepard Company
A Division of William Morrow and Company, Inc.
New York

ALSO BY MELVIN BERGER

The Clarinet and Saxophone Book
The Flute Book
Masters of Modern Music
Jobs That Save Our Environment
Jobs in Fine Arts and Humanities

Copyright © 1978 by Melvin Berger
All rights reserved. No part of this book may be reproduced or utilized in any form or by any means, electronic or mechanical, including photocopying, recording or by any information storage and retrieval system, without permission in writing from the Publisher. Inquiries should be addressed to Lothrop, Lee & Shepard Company, 105 Madison Ave., New York, N. Y. 10016.
Printed in the United States of America.
First Edition
1 2 3 4 5 6 7 8 9 10

Library of Congress Cataloging in Publication Data
Berger, Melvin.
   The trumpet book.

   SUMMARY: Introduces the history and construction of the trumpet, related instruments, composers, musicians, and music written for the trumpet and offers the beginning player advice on instruction and careers.
   1. Trumpet—Juvenile literature. [1. Trumpet]
I. Title.
ML3930.A2B51   788'.1   78-863
ISBN 0-688-41832-5
ISBN 0-688-51832-X lib. bdg.

For Arthur Salz—dear friend and enthusiastic amateur trumpeter

Acknowledgments

Many trumpet players, teachers, and makers helped me with the writing of this book. I thank all of them. I wish, however, to express particular gratitude to players Robert Nagel, Don Smithers, Charles Gouse, and Jesse Levine; to makers Gary Sigurdson and Douglas D. Schneider (Conn), Paul M. Mork (Selmer), Charles A. Ford (Getzen), Vera Cailliet (Leblanc) and William W. Chaloner (Norlin); and to David Baldwin of the International Trumpet Guild.

Contents

1 · The Story of the Trumpet   11
2 · Science and the Trumpet   31
3 · How the Trumpet is Made   42
4 · The Trumpet Family   61
5 · Trumpet Players   76
6 · Trumpet Music   94
7 · You and the Trumpet   104
    Glossary   119
    The Trumpet on Records   123
    Index   127

The business end of a trumpet, one of the most exciting and familiar of all musical instruments.
PHOTOGRAPH SOL GOLDBERG, COURTESY CORNELL UNIVERSITY

1

The Story of the Trumpet

The exciting tone of the trumpet is one of the most familiar sounds of music. Whether it sings out over an entire orchestra or band with its soaring melodies, whether it leads a small Dixieland jazz group or the entire brass section of a big band, whether it is heard in a solo recital in a concert hall or is used to play taps in a distant Army base, everyone knows the brilliant sound of the trumpet.

The appearance of the trumpet is as familiar to us as its sound. Basically, it is a narrow tube of brass metal, about 4 feet long. The tube is doubled over twice to make it easier to handle. At one end is the separate mouthpiece, which supports the player's lips as they vibrate and produce the sound. In the middle are the three valves, which help the player to sound different notes. And at the other end, the tube becomes much wider to form the bell, which projects the sound.

With their bells up high,
the brilliant sound of the six trumpets rings
out over the United States Army Field Band.
COURTESY U.S. ARMY

Today's trumpet is one of the world's oldest instruments. It is the result of many, many centuries of development. Although it looks nothing like its ancestors, there are many similarities. They are all hollow tubes. They are all blown. And they all use the player's lips to produce the basic sound.

The trumpet developed as players and makers worked to improve its design, size, shape, material, and method of construction. They wanted to create an instrument which would produce a beautiful and attractive tone, enable the performer to play all the notes of the scale, extend the range higher and lower, make it possible to play more difficult music, and, in general, be easier to play well. The remarkable way in which the modern trumpet achieves these goals is a measure of the success of all those who struggled to perfect this glorious instrument.

The trumpet is actually the leading member of an entire family of related instruments. There are trumpets of several different sizes, and in several different keys. There are cornets, cornetts, bugles, flugelhorns, and a number of others that are all similar to the trumpet in the way they are made and played.

The trumpet family is much more than a group of related instruments that stir us with their sound, or narrow tubes of metal capable of producing a variety of musical sounds. It is a link that connects us to many different periods of history and to people of many cultures. From the use of trumpets in ancient religious ceremonies to the part they play in modern rock bands, the trumpet family of instruments has much to tell us about civilization and its development.

ORIGIN OF THE TRUMPET

No one will ever know for sure who played the first trumpet, or what the instrument looked like. But it is now believed that the first trumpet originated from a tree branch that had been hollowed out by some kind of insect. The earliest players did not use these hollow tubes to produce musical sounds. Instead, they used them to make the sound of their voices louder. They sang or roared into one end of the tube so that they could be heard at great distances.

Over the centuries, people found that they could also produce loud sounds by singing into other kinds of hollow bodies. Animal horns, bones, sea shells, and grass stems were used as variations of the hollow branch sound-producer.

Also in ancient times, a player discovered that a sound could be made just by blowing through the lips held tightly against a

This old engraving shows a conch shell trumpet that can be traced back to the first time someone produced a sound by blowing a sea animal out of its shell.

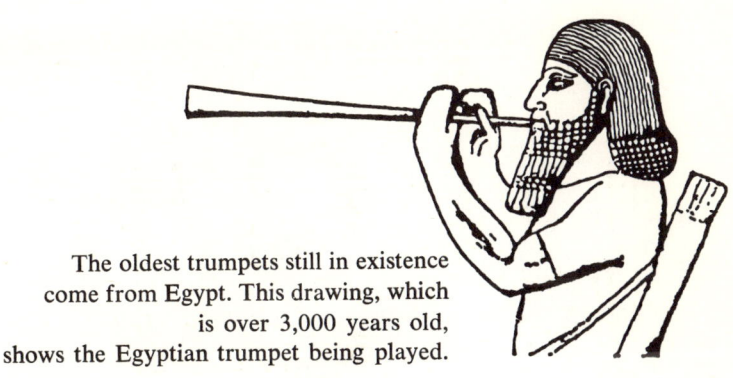

The oldest trumpets still in existence come from Egypt. This drawing, which is over 3,000 years old, shows the Egyptian trumpet being played.

tube. Scholars guess that someone stumbled upon this fact while trying to blow a sea animal out of a shell. This may have been the first time that it was realized that sound could be produced by the lips alone.

The sound of the lips was made louder by being blown through a tube. In time, though, it was found that the sound could be made still louder by making the end of the tube wider. An animal horn or a gourd was attached to the end of the tube. It increased the volume of the original sound. A hollow tube, with a flare or bell at one end, thus became the basis of the trumpet.

An instrument similar to this ancient trumpet is still played today among some primitive tribes in Australia. They call it a **didjeridoo.** It is usually made of a branch of the gum tree. The players produce the sound by using their lips and humming into the tube at the same time. The didjeridoo can be heard on an old recording, *The Land of the Morning Star,* on the British H.M.V. label.

THE FIRST TRUMPETS

The oldest account of a trumpet, in the Epic of Gilgamesh, dates back to about the year 2000 B.C. This story of the legendary Sumerian hero describes how he made a trumpet out of a hollow tree branch, with a wider length of hollow branch attached at one end.

The most ancient trumpets in existence, one silver and one bronze, date back to around 1353 B.C. They were found in the tomb of King Tutankhamen in Egypt. About 23 inches long, they were played with the player's lips held against the narrow end of the tube, without a separate mouthpiece.

Both of these Egyptian trumpets are in such good condition that they have been played by modern players. They are of great historic interest. But musically they are limited. Lacking a mouthpiece, they can produce only two notes, and these are not very attractive in sound.

In the 5th century B.C., the Greek historian Herodotus compared the sound of an Egyptian trumpet to the braying of an ass. In fact, for a good part of their history, trumpets were not played for the beauty of their sound at all. They were used as military signals. They were also used to frighten enemies in battle. Or they were used for religious services and processions. From every description, we learn that the sounds of these early instruments were quite harsh and ugly.

THE TRUMPET IN BIBLICAL TIMES

The trumpet is mentioned many times in the Old Testament of the Bible. This suggests the great significance of the instrument for the people of that period. There is an account in the Bible of two trumpetlike instruments that were used by the Jewish people. They both date back to before the year 1000 B.C. One, the **shofar,** is still in use today. It is made of an animal horn, and is only blown on special holidays. The other, the **hatzotzeroth,** is described in the Book of Numbers as part of a divine command to Moses: "Make thee two trumpets of

The shofar is the oldest ancestor of the trumpet that is still played. It is used on special Jewish holidays.
PHOTOGRAPH MELVIN BERGER

silver; of a whole piece shalt thou make them: that thou mayest use them for the calling of the assembly, and for the journeying of the camps." The instrument was held in such honor that it was written in another place that God commanded Moses: "Speak unto the children of Israel, saying, 'In the seventh month, in the first day of the month, shall ye have a sabbath, a memorial of blowing of trumpets, an holy convocation.'"

According to the Jewish historian Flavius Josephus (37-95 A.D.), the hatzotzeroth was a straight tube, about 20 inches long, with a bell at the end. From his telling, we understand that it looked very much like the Egyptian trumpet.

This engraving by Arnold van Westerhout, from 1716, shows the ancient Jewish trumpet, the hatzotzeroth.

The hatzotzerothim (plural) played a very important part in the life of the Jewish people—both in their military and religious activity. Between 1400 and 1200 B.C., Joshua and the Israelite trumpet players marched around the walls guarding the city of Jericho, until, the Bible relates, the "wall fell down flat." Although modern research indicates that it was an earthquake, and not Joshua's trumpets that flattened the walls of Jericho, the fact that the trumpet is said to have been involved in this significant victory against the Philistines is in itself noteworthy. Josephus estimated that, in the time of King Solomon, there were 200,000 trumpet players in the land of Israel. One hundred and twenty trumpeters played at the consecration of Solomon's holy temple.

THE TRUMPETS OF ANCIENT GREECE AND ROME

A Greek trumpet, called a **salpinx**, can be seen at the Museum of Fine Arts in Boston. It is a 62-inch, straight tube, making it longer than the Egyptian and Jewish instruments. The Boston salpinx, dating from the 5th century B.C., is made of 13 separate sections of ivory joined by rings of bronze, with a wide bell, also of bronze. Playing this instrument must have been quite an accomplishment, because salpinx contests were an important part of the Olympic Games of ancient Greece. Nevertheless, the sound was described by the Greek poet Aeschylus as "yelling."

In the Roman civilization that began around 300 B.C., and followed that of the Greeks, legions of soldiers provided the military power that made the Roman Empire great. When besieging new territory or repelling attacks from invaders, the Roman soldiers used several kinds of trumpets. The Roman **tuba,** which is nothing like our modern tuba, was the instrument of the marching soldiers, the infantry. It looks like a slightly smaller version of the salpinx. The tuba in the Etruscan Museum in Rome, Italy, is a straight bronze tube, about 46 inches long, with a bell at the end.

The instrument of the riding Roman soldiers, the cavalry, was the **lituus.** The lituus is shaped like the letter J. It was played with the curved section facing upwards. The shape is obviously a metal version of a hollow reed trumpet with an animal horn attached as a bell. A lituus from the time of Julius Caesar, just over 63 inches long, can be seen at the Vatican Museum in Rome.

The Roman trumpet players blew into these large hollow metal instruments with great force. They puffed out their cheeks to get even more pressure. To help support their cheeks, they wore a leather head and face band called a capistrum.

Neither the tuba or the lituus had a very agreeable sound. This is not surprising, since the main use of the trumpets here, too, was to signal the Roman soldiers and to frighten the enemy. Accounts from the time describe the instruments' tones as horrible, rude, and shrieklike.

TRUMPETS IN THE MIDDLE AGES

Around 400 A.D., the Roman Empire became so weak that it fell to the barbarian tribes from the North. This period, when Europe fell under the control of these tribes, is called the Middle Ages. It lasted until about 1500.

During the Middle Ages, most of western Europe was divided into large estates called manors. These manors were ruled by powerful lords. Knights defended the lords, and serfs or peasants farmed the land. The lords lived in mighty stone castles. Lords, ladies, and knights feasted in huge banquet halls and were entertained by wandering poets and musicians.

Tromba Romana antica.

The marching Roman soldiers used this trumpet, which they called the tuba.

The trumpet of the Roman riding soldiers
was the lituus, shown here
in a Westerhout engraving.

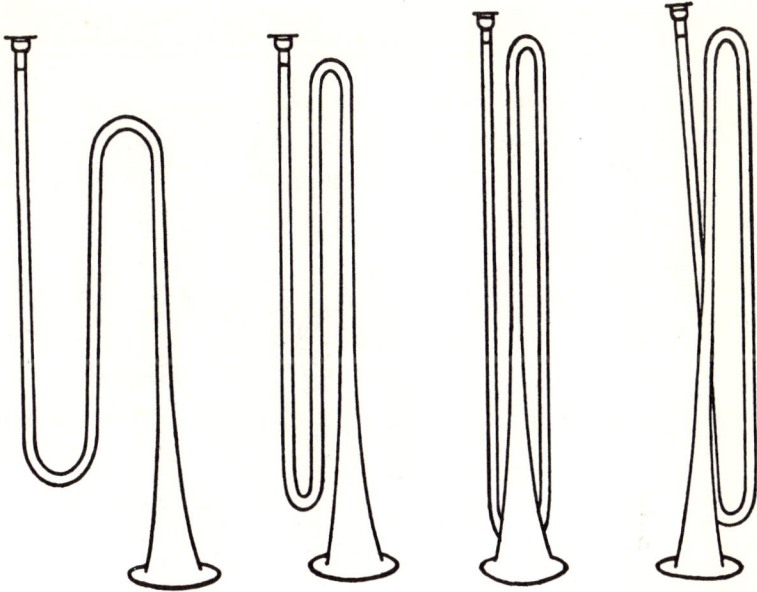

During the Middle Ages the straight trumpet was folded over in several stages until it reached its final shape.

In this period, trumpets were first used to play melodies, and not just as instruments to sound signals or calls to battle. Paintings and writings from that time show the trumpets as straight metal tubes. They varied in length from about 2 feet to about 6 feet.

The longer one, called **busine,** was the better instrument. It was named after a large, coiled Roman horn, the *buccina.* The busine was able to play more notes than the shorter trumpets. By the year 1300, the busine was folded into a flat S-shape, instead of a straight pipe.

Trumpeters worked for the aristocrats—the kings, lords, princes, dukes, and barons—that ruled the manors all over Europe. These trumpet players were considered servants of the court, and their duties included waiting on tables. But they were servants of high rank. In fact, they often had other servants who worked for them.

It was the job of the trumpet player to announce the presence of the aristocrats in processions and at festivals. The more trumpeters you had to announce your approach and herald your entrance, the greater your power and position were considered to be.

In the year 1426, King Sigismund (1368–1437), King of Germany and later Emperor of the Holy Roman Empire, broke the hold that nobles had on all trumpet players. In return for a large contribution, he permitted the city of Augsburg to hire town trumpeters. Other towns quickly won similar permission. The number of trumpet players employed in these towns increased.

Towns in the Middle Ages were small settlements around a castle or a church. The towns kept growing larger and larger. Walls were built around them. Soldiers were posted on the walls and on tall church towers to keep watch for attacking armies. These trumpeters were called the *Thurmer*, or tower trumpeters. At the approach of an enemy, they played a warning signal for the townspeople.

Another group of trumpeters was called the *Stadtpfeifer*, or town pipers. They played for occasions of state, as well as for feasts and celebrations.

Both groups of trumpeters were organized into guilds. The guilds protected their members by setting prices and wages for services. They settled disputes between trumpeters and employers. They also limited the number of players, and confined the secrets of trumpet playing to a carefully chosen few.

THE NATURAL TRUMPET

By the year 1500, the trumpet had taken the shape and form it was to keep for the next 300 years. It was known as the natural trumpet. It was about 7 feet long, and was usually folded over in one long loop. Sometimes it was made in a coiled, circular shape. The metal tube was about 4/10ths of an inch wide, opening up to a 4-inch bell at one end. In fact, it resembled today's trumpet, though longer and without valves. Usually made of brass or silver, the tubing of the natural trumpet was highly decorated with carvings and ornamental cords.

Johann Sebastian Bach and George Frideric Handel composed music in the first half of the 18th century for the natural trumpet. In many of their orchestral works, the trumpet part adds a festive brilliance to the entire composition. Music of praise or glory rings out with splendid clarity. This bright melodic style is known as *clarino playing*.

A great deal of confusion surrounds the clarino style. Many attempts have been made over the years to reproduce the clarino style with modern instruments. Trumpets built to play clarino parts are called Bach trumpets, piccolo trumpets, or high trumpets.

Actually, the clarino players of Bach's day used the ordinary natural trumpet. There was the 8-foot-long instrument, which was pitched in C, and the 7-foot instrument, pitched in D. Of the two, the 7-foot D trumpet was the more popular.

The long, narrow tube of the natural trumpet made it possible to play very high notes. A very shallow mouthpiece also favored the production of high notes. A number of fine trumpet players specialized in performing the high clarino parts. These highly skilled clarino performers concentrated on the high notes, and spent many hours of daily practice in developing this ability. They became so specialized that they were unable to play the lower notes that could also be produced on the natural trumpet using different mouthpieces.

As a result, the large range of the instrument was divided

into four parts: clarino, second clarino, *tromba*, and *principale*. A trumpet player in Bach's day was an expert in one of these. A few specialized in the highest part, the clarino. Some excelled in the next lowest part, the second clarino. The part beneath the second clarino was the *tromba*, which is the Italian word for trumpet. The *tromba*'s range was roughly the same as the lower part of the range of the modern trumpet. And the lowest part, the *principale*, went down 8 notes lower than the *tromba*. All these parts were performed on 7-foot trumpets, but each specialist used a different mouthpiece to help produce his own special range of notes.

THE SLIDE TRUMPET

Although it was never as popular as the natural trumpet, the slide trumpet was played from the 15th century to the beginning of the 20th century. The slide trumpet developed from the straight medieval trumpet. The tube was lengthened and doubled over. A mouthpiece with a particularly long neck was used. To play the instrument, the player slid the entire trumpet, called a **trompette des menéstrel,** back and forth on the mouthpiece neck. When the player pulled it out slightly, the pitch dropped a half tone. When it was pulled out further, it dropped a full tone.

A slide trumpet from 1651 is in the museum of the Berlin High School for Music in Berlin, Germany. The mouthpiece neck of this instrument is 22 inches long. It allowed the player to go down two whole tones. The best-known music for this instrument was written in the following century by Johann Sebastian Bach. He called the instrument **tromba da tirarsi,** which means slide trumpet in Italian.

After Bach's death, few composers wrote for the slide trumpet. It was seldom played, except in England. Here a slide

The slide trumpet player slips the entire instrument back and forth along the neck of the mouthpiece, as seen in this 1716 engraving.

trumpet designed by John Hyde continued to be used until 1900 or so. It has not been revived because it is awkward to hold, and hard to play. But most of all, it has not come back because the notes it produces are badly out of tune.

THE AGE OF MECHANIZATION

Clarino playing declined by the end of the 18th century. The French Revolution hastened its fall from popularity by putting an end to the many small courts that supported and encouraged trumpet playing. The very powerful trumpet guilds prevented widespread study and performance of the trumpet. And the growth of orchestras hurried the drop in the trumpet's popularity. In the large orchestras, the clarino part, which sounded best when played softly, had to be played loudly to be heard. Loud playing produced an ugly sound. Composers who were writing symphonies for the new orchestras ceased writing melodies for the trumpet. They confined the instrument to playing just a few notes, mostly to add fullness to the sound of the entire orchestra.

At about this time, a different kind of trumpet came into popular use. It was the natural trumpet, but the curved section, where the tubing was bent over, could be removed. This curved section is called a *crook*. Each trumpet was equipped with several crooks of different lengths. By using shorter or longer crooks, the player was able to raise or lower the pitch of the entire trumpet. Each crook changed the key of the trumpet, and made it possible to play more notes than could be played without crooks. However, the main difficulty with using crooks was that players had to stop, remove the old crook, and insert a new one before going on to play notes in a different key.

With the end of clarino playing and the clumsiness of the

crooks, trumpet playing was at a low point. But there was so much pressure from players and makers, and composers too, for an improved instrument that it spurred on a great upsurge in experiments and attempts to create better trumpets. These efforts to perfect the trumpet resulted in many improvements. Perhaps the most important improvement was the invention of *valves*. For the first time, valves allowed a good, reliable, fast, in-tune way to play different notes on the trumpet, without depending entirely on the player's lips or the awkward crooks.

The first patent for a trumpet with two valves was taken out in Berlin in 1818 by Heinrich Stölzel and Friedrich Blühmel. Stölzel was the first horn player in the Royal Opera Orchestra of Berlin; Blühmel played the oboe in an amateur band organized by a coal-mining company. Each man insisted that he had invented the valve. There is no hard evidence for one or the other. But the accepted belief today is that Stölzel was the first to think of the valve, and Blühmel was the first to build one.

The valve patent was sold to the instrument makers, Griessling and Schlott, in Berlin. The first instruments that they produced had two valves. But the instruments were not very good. Consequently, most German trumpeters did not switch over to these new valved instruments. In Russia, France, and Austria, however, players quickly accepted the valved trumpets.

Meanwhile, other musicians began to perfect the two-valved instruments. In 1824, John Shaw, an English trumpet player, enhanced the action of the valves by adding springs to the mechanism. A few years later, C. A. Müller in Germany added a third valve, similar to today's trumpet. And, in 1839, François Perinet produced a valve that is essentially the same as the one used on trumpets today.

The valves made it possible to shorten the tube length of the trumpet to 4 feet, and still play a wide range of notes. As a full-fledged melodic instrument, the valved trumpet was welcomed into the orchestra. The first well-known parts for valved trumpets were written in opera scores. Jacques Halévy wrote parts for valved trumpets in his 1835 opera, *La Juive*, and Giacomo Meyerbeer used them in *Les Huguenots* the following year.

Since then, the modern valved trumpet has won a place for itself in every symphony and opera orchestra, in every marching, concert, and jazz band, and as an important chamber music and solo instrument.

To understand more fully the revolutionary development of the trumpet from a limited, harsh-sounding instrument, to a melodious, clear music maker, it will help to know exactly how the trumpet works, and how the valves help it to work better.

2

Science and the Trumpet

All sound is vibration. The trumpet and all other musical instruments produce their sounds because something is set into vibration. Things that vibrate shake back and forth very rapidly. On the violin, the string vibrates. On the drum, it is the drum head. And on the trumpet, it is the player's lips.

BUZZING LIPS

If you don't think that your lips can be set into vibration to produce a sound, try this. Hold your lips firmly together. Pull the corners of your mouth back towards your ears as though you were smiling. Now, with your lips tight against your teeth, blow out a narrow jet of air between your lips, at the center.

The buzzing sound that you hear is made by your vibrating lips. The sound need not stay the same. If you wish, it can go up in pitch. To change the pitch of the buzz, you need to make your lips vibrate faster. One way to increase the speed of vibrations is to tighten your lips even more. Press two fingers on your lips about one inch apart. Pull back the corners of your mouth, and buzz again with your lips. Did the pitch go up? Your fingers support and tighten your lips so that they can vibrate faster. The faster the vibrations, the higher the pitch.

This experiment with a balloon can show how air sets lips into vibration. Blow up the balloon. Open the neck of the balloon and let a narrow column of air escape through the opening. Listen to the sound made by the escaping air.

The blown-up balloon is like a trumpet player's lungs filled with air. The opening is like the player's lips. As the air inside the balloon (lungs) rushes out, it sets the opening (lips) into vibration and produces sound.

Blow the balloon up again. Now, stretch the opening making it wider, but more narrow. Let some air escape. Do you hear the pitch of the sound go up? The stretched balloon opening (tighter lips) increases the speed of the vibrations.

The slowly released air sets the player's lips into vibration. The vibrating lips create a buzz. But breath and vibrating lips alone do not produce the glorious sound of the trumpet. The buzz must be combined with the 4-foot column of air in the tube of the trumpet to produce a musical sound.

INSIDE THE TRUMPET

When the player blows into the trumpet, the air from the lungs sets the lips into vibration. But it also creates a disturbance in the tube. It sets the air inside the tube vibrating. The tiny particles of air are set into very fast, very tiny, back-and-forth movement. These vibrating air particles form a pattern, a wave, that runs from one end of the trumpet to the other.

When the player blows with loose, relaxed lips, a single

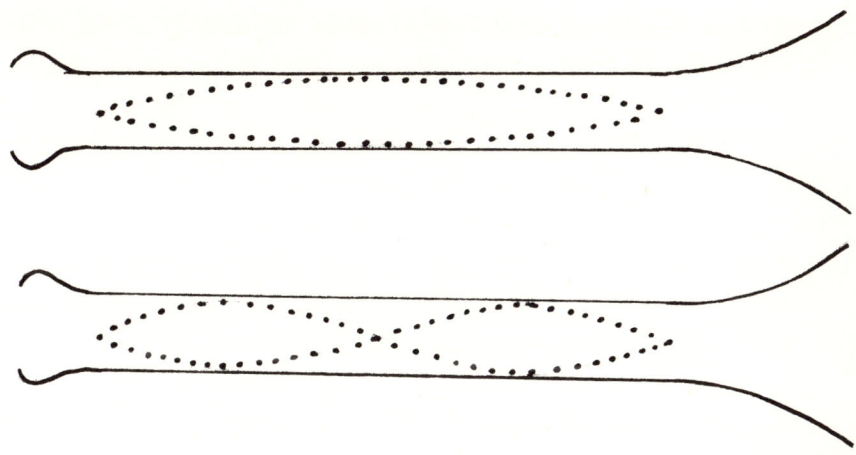

If you could see the vibrating air inside a trumpet, you would see a single wave form when the player blows with loose, relaxed lips. With tighter lips and more powerful breath, the single wave breaks into two or more waves.

wave forms in the trumpet. Near the player's lips, the air in the tube does not vibrate at all. The vibrations get stronger and stronger farther along the tube. At the center of the tube, they are strongest and widest. The air vibrates less and less strongly near the bell. At the bell, there is no vibration. The points of no vibration at both ends are the *nodes*. The point of greatest vibration in the middle of the tube is the *antinode*.

This particular pattern of vibrations, a single wave, produces the lowest note on the trumpet. It is called the *fundamental note* of the instrument.

When the player tightens his or her lips and blows slightly harder, it creates faster vibrations in the trumpet. A different pattern of vibrations forms. The single wave breaks in half, becoming two separate waves. Each new wave vibrates twice as fast as the single wave. Since there are now two waves, there are nodes at both ends, as well as at the center of the tube. There are anti-nodes one-quarter and three-quarters of the way along the tube.

This pattern of vibrations produces a higher-pitched note. In fact, the pitch is exactly eight notes, or an *octave*, higher than the fundamental note. It is called the *first overtone*.

By further tightening the lips and blowing slightly harder, the player breaks the single wave into three separate waves within the trumpet tube. Now there are four nodes with three anti-nodes between them. The pitch of this note is exactly an octave plus five notes above the fundamental note. It is five notes above the first overtone. It is called the *second overtone*.

As the player tightens the lips and blows still harder, the wave breaks into more and more sections. Each tone that is produced is several notes higher than the one before. These notes, coming from the increasing number of waves inside the trumpet, make up the *overtone series*.

The vibrations of the overtones are always two, three, four, five, or more times the vibrations of the fundamental note. In other words, if the basic note vibrates 100 times per second, the overtones would vibrate 200, 300, 400, 500 or more times per second. The greater the speed of vibration, the higher the pitch.

The distances between the first few notes of the overtone series are quite large. There are eight notes between the fundamental and the first overtone; five notes between the first and the second overtones; four notes between the second and third. The higher the notes in the overtone series, the closer together they are in pitch. Trumpet players who only use their vibrating lips to change pitch can only play the notes in the overtone series. They cannot play the notes in-between. They cannot play a scale or most melodies.

The **bugle** is an instrument in the trumpet family that only uses the player's lips to change pitch. It can only sound the notes in the overtone series. About the only music that you can play on the bugle are calls, such as *Taps* and *Reveille*. If you hum these calls to yourself, you will hear how they skip from note to note. That is because the bugle can only sound these few notes.

By contrast, the story of the development of the trumpet focuses on attempts throughout history to make an instrument that could play *all* the notes of a scale. One early solution, described in Chapter 1, was to build a trumpet with a long pipe and a shallow mouthpiece. This instrument was used for the clarino parts. The clarino player could play high in the overtone series, where the notes are close together. It was, therefore, possible to play high-pitched melodies and scales.

VALVES

A greater range of notes was made possible by the addition of valves, producing the trumpet in use today. Each valve adds a different length of tubing to the basic length of the trumpet. The three valves are lined up on the section of pipe in line with the mouthpiece.

Attached to the trumpet's first valve is a length of tubing that is about $6\frac{1}{2}$ inches long. When the player blows into the instrument without pressing the valve, the air bypasses this extra length. But when the player presses the valve, the air is sent through the extra pipe. This makes the vibrating length of the tube longer. The longer the tube, the greater the wave length. And the longer the wave length, the lower the pitch.

The extra length of tubing lowers the pitch exactly one whole step. For example, suppose the player sounds the note C by blowing into the trumpet. By blowing again, and without

The valve can be removed from the trumpet. When it is pressed down, the air passes through an extra length of tubing.
PHOTOGRAPH ELEANOR BERGER

changing either the tightness of the lips or the pressure of the breath, the player can drop the note to B♭, a whole step beneath C.

The second valve is connected to about 3½ inches of tubing, which is about half as long as the tubing on the first valve. Pressing the second valve drops the pitch a half step.

Suppose the player sounding the note C presses the second valve, without changing the lip or breath pressure. The pitch now goes down to B natural, a half step below C.

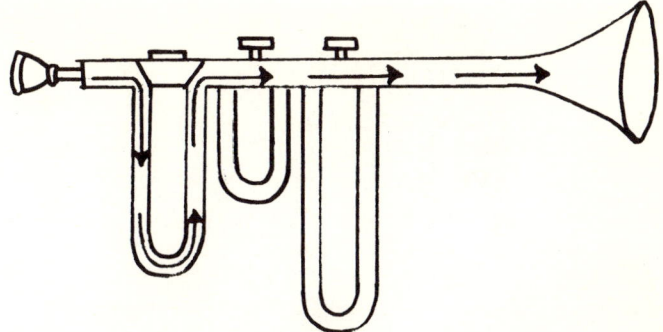

This diagram shows what happens when the first valve is pressed down.

The tubing attached to the third valve is longest of all. It is nearly 10½ inches in length. Since it is nearly as long as the first and second valves combined, it lowers the pitch one and a half steps.

The three valves may be used individually or in combination. For instance, here is how the player goes down a scale in half steps, just by using the valves. The player blows with no valves down. Pressing only the second valve lowers the pitch a half step. Pressing only the first valve lowers the pitch a whole step. The first and second together, or only the third, lowers the pitch one and a half steps. The second and third together lower the pitch two steps. The first and third together lower the pitch two and a half steps. And all three valves together lower the pitch three whole steps.

By using the valves in this way, and by using lips and breath to get the different notes of the overtone series, the player is able to produce the range of notes in a scale.

TUNING

The valves and the overtone series make it possible to play

By pulling out the tuning slide the player lengthens the tubing and lowers the pitch.
PHOTOGRAPH ELEANOR BERGER

many different notes on the trumpet. But they do not solve the problem of pitch. In a band or orchestra, the player must be able to adjust the trumpet's pitch as high or just as low as the other instruments.

To do this, the player pulls out or pushes in the *tuning slide*. This is a U-shaped length of tubing at the first curve in the trumpet tube. Pulling it out lengthens the overall trumpet tube, and therefore lowers the pitch slightly. Pushing it in shortens the length, and thus raises the pitch a little.

A similar, though smaller, tuning slide is attached to the third valve of most good trumpets. When all three valves, or the first and third valves are pressed, the notes sound out of tune. They are a bit too high in pitch. A tuning slide on the third valve, and sometimes on the first valve as well, allows the player to produce these notes in tune. The player slips a finger of the right hand through the loop on these slides. If a note sounds too high, he or she pulls out a slide, lengthening the sound wave and lowering the pitch.

Attached to the tuning slides are the *water keys.* They are used to get rid of water that collects in the trumpet tubing. As water vapor in the player's breath touches the cold metal of the trumpet tube, it condenses and becomes liquid water. (It is pure water that collects, not saliva, as some people think!) Since the water can interfere with the trumpet tone, the player wants to remove it from the instrument. By opening the water keys, which are in the bottom curve of the two tuning slides, and by shaking the trumpet, the player allows any water that has accumulated to drip out.

MUTES

Mutes are separate devices that are inserted into the bell of the trumpet. They change the quality of the tone, or the *tone color.* The player has a variety of mutes to choose from. Each one produces a different tone color.

The most popular mute, and the most commonly used in symphony playing, is the *straight mute.* It looks like an empty ice-cream cone with the tip cut off. The straight mute, like most of the others, is made either of metal, plastic, or a fiber composition similar to masonite. The straight mute softens the basic trumpet tone. It also adds a slightly nasal quality.

Other mutes are mainly used in popular music. Jazz players frequently use a *cup* mute. It gives the trumpet a softer, more mellow sound. The cup mute also looks like a cone, but with a very large scoop of ice cream. The rounded "scoop" sur-

The straight mute is inserted into the bell of the trumpet to soften the tone.
PHOTOGRAPH ELEANOR BERGER

rounds the opening of the cone and extends out on all sides.

The *Harmon* or "Wa-Wah" *mute* is another jazz mute. It resembles the cup mute, except that it has a plunger right through the middle. By pushing the plunger in and out with the left hand, the player is able to get a changing, "wa-wah," quality of tone.

Jazz musicians use other mutes for certain special effects. The *derby mute* is nothing more than a derby hat that is either held in front of the bell, or hung over the bell. It gives

As the player waves his hand in front of the Harmon mute, he produces a "wa-wah" sound.
PHOTOGRAPH MELVIN BERGER

the trumpet a softer, slightly more mellow tone color. The *plunger* is a rubber gadget similar to the plunger that is used to clear clogged drains. Trumpet players use it to give an edge to their tone, or for a "wa-wah" effect. The *buzz mute* gives the player's tone a buzz or a "wow" sound, depending on how it is used. There are also several varieties of straight and cup mutes made of different materials that change the basic trumpet sound.

The player's lips, the mouthpiece, the length of tubing, the valves, and the mutes are essential to the working of the trumpet. Although simple in construction, the modern trumpet can produce some of the most varied and powerful sounds of any musical instrument.

3

How the Trumpet is Made

A trumpet factory is a place where workers transform lengths of dull brass tubes and sheets of metal into gleaming trumpets capable of producing the most beautiful of musical sounds. The story of how metal worth about $1 is changed into an instrument worth up to $600 is the story of how trumpets are made.

SHAPING THE TUBING

Brass, the basic metal of trumpets, is a mixture, or alloy, of two metals. It is mostly copper, with some zinc. The most common alloy contains about 70% copper and about 30% zinc. This mixture is called yellow brass. A few instruments, though, are made from gold or red brass, which contain as much as 85% copper and only 15% zinc. In general, a higher percentage of copper means a more mellow tone, while a higher percentage of zinc produces a more brilliant sound.

Heavy rolls of sheet brass are cut to make the various parts of the trumpet.
COURTESY THE SELMER COMPANY, ELKHART, INDIANA

The brass arrives at the factory as long, narrow tubes or cylinders, usually 0.45 inches in diameter, or as heavy rolls of sheet brass. Although the sheets of brass are very thin, usually 28/1,000ths of an inch, a roll of sheet metal weighs hundreds of pounds.

Each factory has its own particular way of shaping the brass tube and the sheet of brass into a trumpet. But in general the first step is to cut the brass tubing for the body of the instrument.

A worker takes a 12-foot length of tubing and cuts it down to the proper length with the sharp blade of a metal saw. The saw slices through the metal with a loud, piercing screech. The tubing then needs to be drawn out until it is tapered, and bent to the correct shape.

In the hand method of forming a curve, the worker stops up one end of the tube, and coats the inside of the tube with grease. Then he or she pours melted lead into the tube. Working slowly by hand, the worker firmly pulls the tube into the right shape. The lead filling prevents the tube from cracking or collapsing. Once the curve is correct, the worker melts out the lead and the hollow tube is bent.

The more modern method, and the one used most widely, is to bend the tube by machine. The machine uses water, or hydraulic pressure, to bend the tube into shape, without damaging the metal in any way.

CUTTING AND SHAPING THE BELL

While one worker is preparing the tubing for the trumpet, another is making the bell of the instrument. When made by hand, workers use a pair of heavy shears or a mechanical knife to cut out a section of flat metal according to a pattern. The flat pattern resembles a battle-ax used by knights in the Middle Ages. By heating and hammering the flat metal, an experienced worker shapes the flat piece of metal into the swelling round curves of a trumpet bell.

However, this operation, too, is most often performed by machine. A giant stamping machine automatically cuts out the

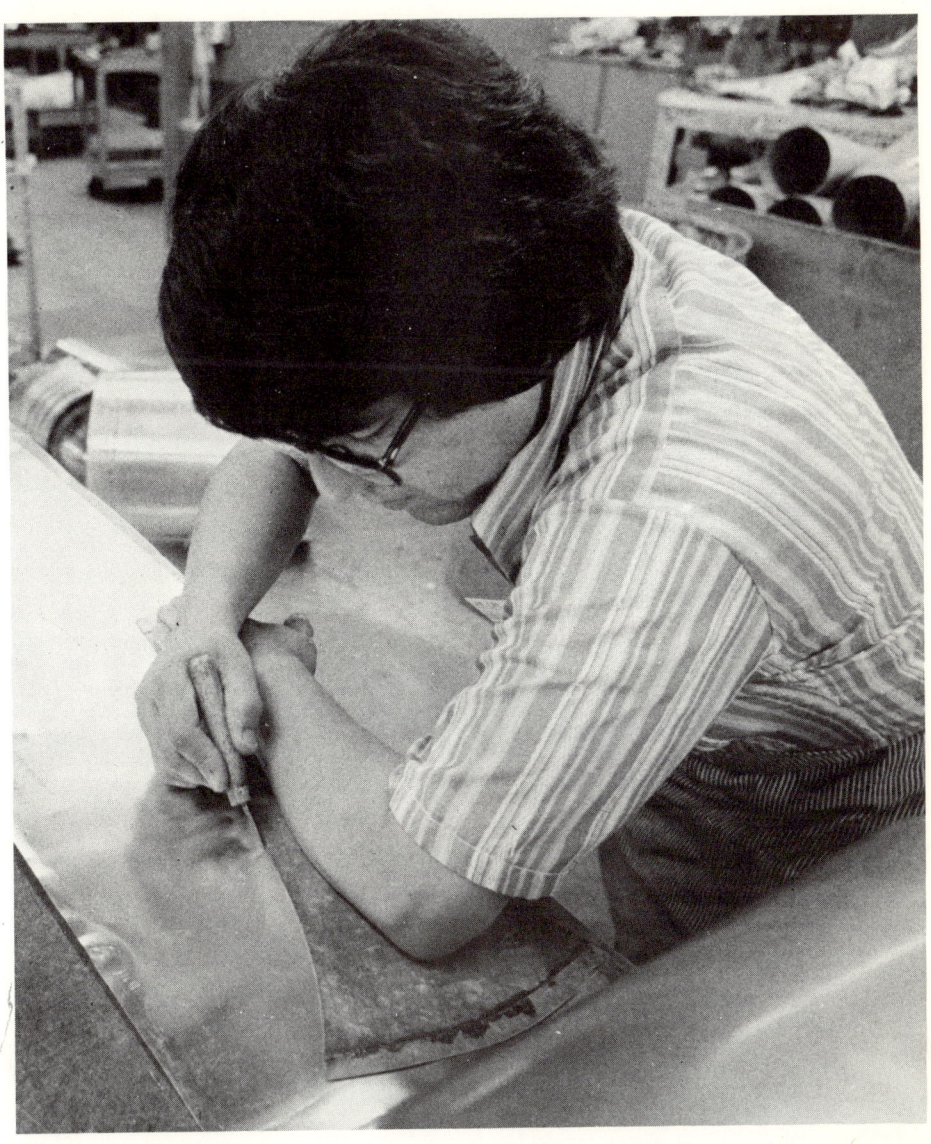

The worker carefully traces the pattern for the bell on the flat brass. This is the first step in the hand process of making a bell.
COURTESY C. G. CONN, LTD.

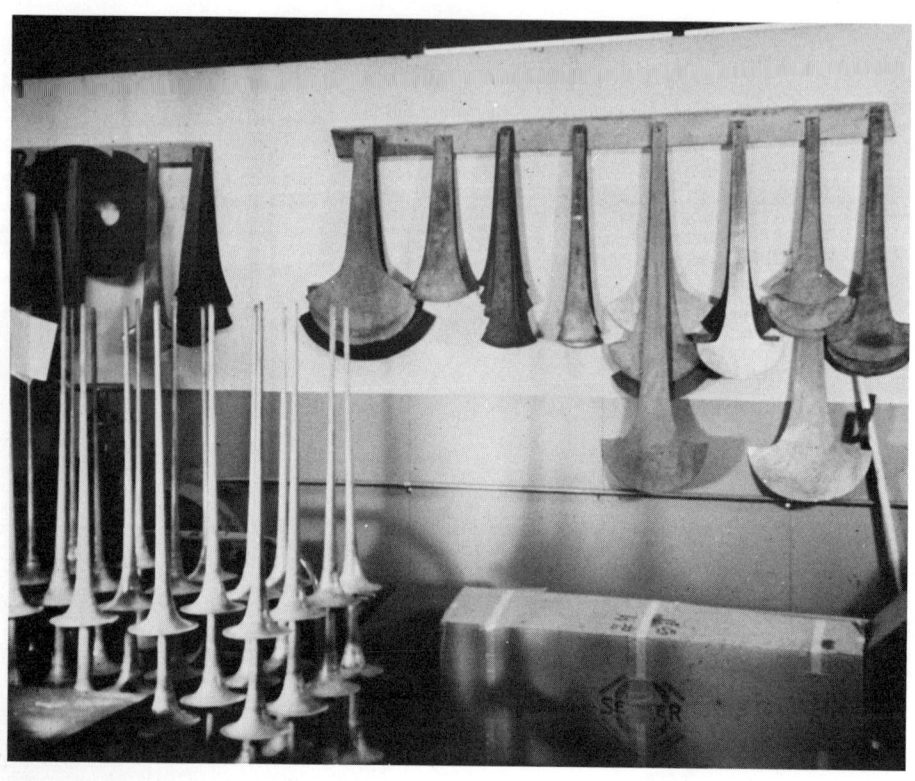

The patterns used to cut out the brass for the bells hang on the walls of the factory. Piles of finished bells are stacked in front.
COURTESY THE SELMER COMPANY, ELKHART, INDIANA

pattern from the sheet metal, and presses it into the right shape. Controlling this machine requires great skill and control. A worker may spend three years as an apprentice learning how to operate this equipment.

The final shaping of the bell is done on a lathe. The brass bell is placed on this tool, which spins around. As it spins, an expert uses a series of wooden shaping wands, a triangular-bladed knife, and an emery cloth to stretch the metal over a

In the hand method, the brass is heated
and hammered into the proper bell shape.
COURTESY THE SELMER COMPANY, ELKHART, INDIANA

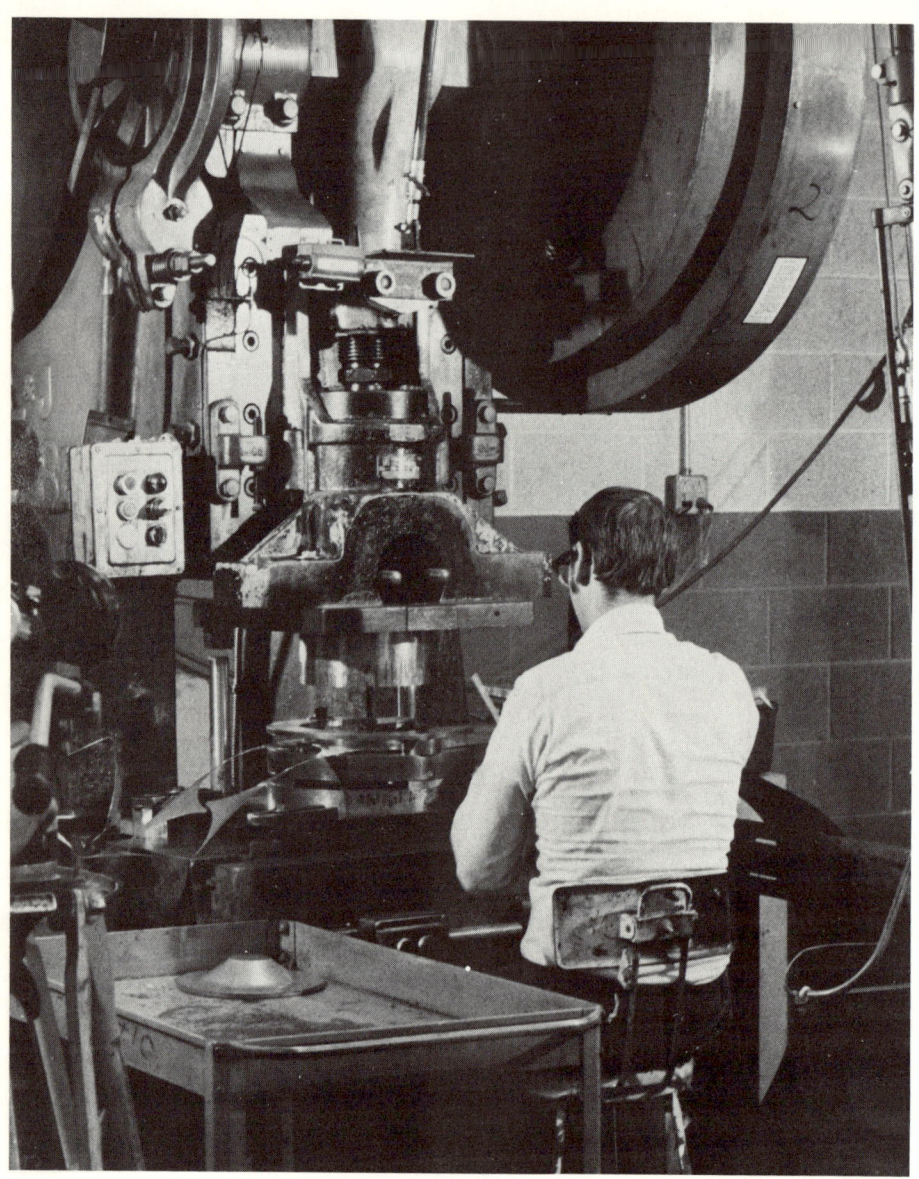

The operator is seated at a giant stamping machine that cuts the brass and shapes the bell.
COURTESY C. G. CONN, LTD.

The final shaping of the bell
is done by spinning it on a lathe.
COURTESY THE SELMER COMPANY, ELKHART, INDIANA

form. The bell flares out into a beautiful soft curve. After spinning, a worker finishes shaping the bell and smoothing out the metal by hand.

The bell receives its graceful shape
on a lathe controlled by
a highly experienced operator.
COURTESY C. G. CONN, LTD.

It takes more hammering to attach the bell to the tubing.
COURTESY THE SELMER COMPANY, ELKHART, INDIANA

SOLDERING THE PARTS

Next the graceful, flared bell is soldered to the tubing. Now the metal begins to look like a trumpet. Little knobs of solder, called "ears," are filed off by hand. And the trumpet-to-be is stacked in a row on the floor to await further additions.

Altogether it takes one hundred and fifty parts to complete a trumpet. The instrument progresses through about a dozen production rooms. At each stop, pieces of brass tubing of different shapes and sizes, which have been cut and shaped in various departments, are added and soldered to the main stem of the trumpet.

It takes about one hundred and fifty parts
to complete a trumpet. Here the worker
is soldering a support brace into place.
COURTESY C. G. CONN, LTD.

The pistons for the valves are made with great care. They must be accurate to within 1/10,000th of an inch.
COURTESY THE SELMER COMPANY, ELKHART, INDIANA

MAKING AND MOUNTING THE VALVES

Most master trumpet makers agree that the valves are the heart of the trumpet. The valves are assembled and attached to the trumpet in the mounting department. While precision and accuracy are essential at every stage of production, they are most crucial in valve-making and valve-mounting. The worker must make the pistons inside the valves no more than 1/10,000ths of an inch away from the walls. That is about 1/30th the width of a human hair!

Some workers in the mounting department join the three valves together by hand. They hold the roaring blue flame of

The valves are dipped into a bath
that plates them with a thin coat of nickel.
COURTESY THE SELMER COMPANY, ELKHART, INDIANA

a very hot torch over the metal casings until they are glowing red hot. With a thin strand of silver wire, they solder the three cases together. The brass linings of the piston openings are also soldered in place by hand to make an airtight seal. The actual valves are prepared by other workers. They are precision ground on very accurate machines to achieve the absolute perfection that is needed.

Sometimes the valves are dipped into a bath that plates them with a thin coat of nickel. The nickel plating prevents corrosion. They are left with a satin, rather than a smooth finish, so that they will be able to hold a coating of oil when they are in use.

After all the separate parts of the trumpet are completed, the assembler joins them together to make the finished instrument.
COURTESY C. G. CONN, LTD.

CLEANING, BUFFING, AND POLISHING

After all the parts are assembled and soldered on to the instrument, the joints are cleaned and smoothed. They are checked to be sure that they are holding correctly. A worker goes over the entire surface looking for any dents, damages, or dirt. With a tool that looks like a large kitchen knife, he or she scrapes away any unwanted material that has become attached to the trumpet.

Before being buffed, any unwanted material
on the instrument is scraped off.
The worker is cleaning this tuba
the same way that he would clean a trumpet.
COURTESY C. G. CONN, LTD.

From the cleaning step, the trumpet goes to the buffing and polishing department. Here it is smoothed on a rapidly spinning belt sander. This machine smooths the metal, but still leaves it rough to the touch.

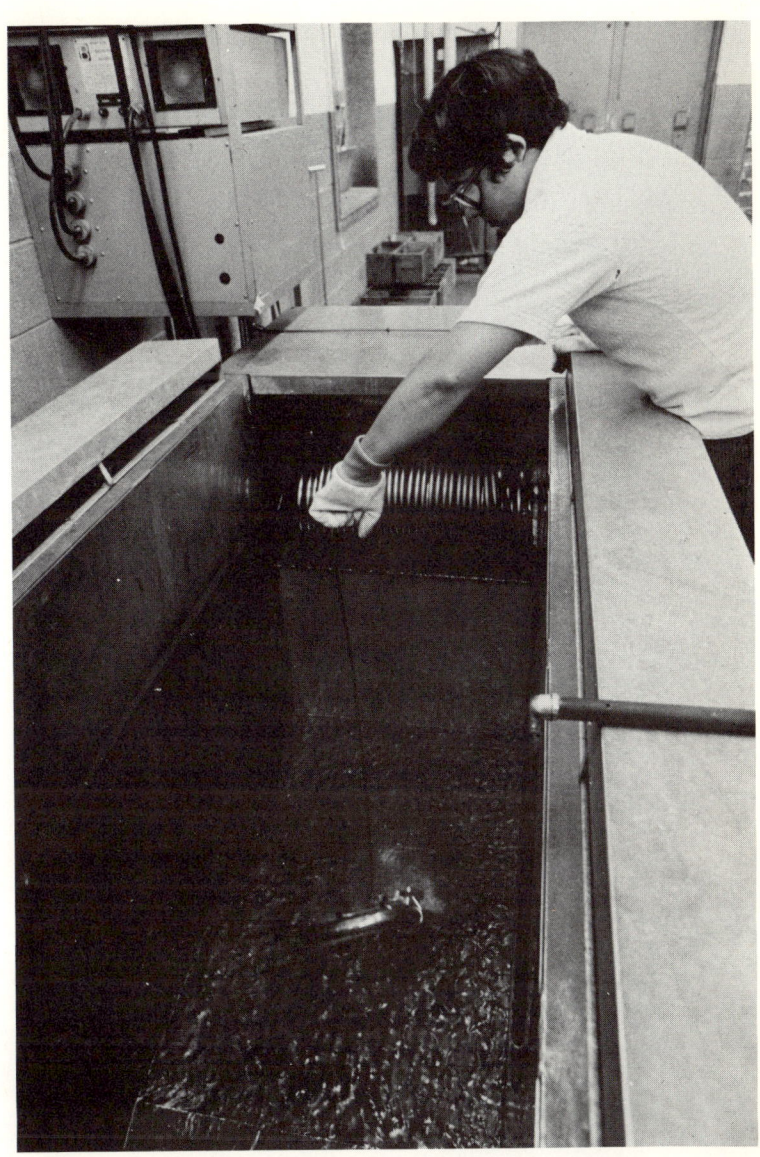

The finished instrument is dipped into a vat of powerful chemicals to remove all traces of dirt and grease.
COURTESY C. G. CONN, LTD.

This is followed by buffing on a hard wheel with a special buffing compound. Finally, the instrument is softly buffed on fluffy cloth wheels with rouge, a fine powder that jewelers use to clean and polish fine gold and silver.

The buffing wheels polish most of the new instrument. But they are not able to reach into every curve of the trumpet. These hard-to-get-at parts must be polished by hand, in a process known as "hand ragging."

After an hour of buffing and polishing, the brass is shiny and gleaming. It is dipped into a vat of chemical fumes which remove all traces of dirt and grease. Then, gloved workers cover the instrument with either a thin lacquer coat on expensive instruments, or a thin layer of transparent plastic on inexpensive ones. Both protect the metal, and give the instrument an attractive, shiny appearance. Instead of the lacquer or plastic coat, a certain number of trumpets are plated with either silver or gold.

FINAL ASSEMBLY AND TESTING

At this point, the trumpet is ready for the final assembly. The pistons, springs, finger buttons, and felt buffers are attached to the valves. The slides are inserted. A cork is glued into the water key.

The trumpet is now finished. But before it is released, the instrument must be tested, inspected and played. In one test, a worker seals the bell, making the instrument airtight. He or she attaches the hose from a vacuum pump to the mouthpiece end of the trumpet. As the vacuum is turned on, the worker holds the trumpet up and listens very carefully. Is there any hiss? If there is a sound, it means that the instrument is not airtight, and it is sent back for correction.

Another inspector checks all the moving parts of the trum-

A final hand cleaning, and the finished trumpet is sealed in a plastic bag to keep it clean.
COURTESY THE SELMER COMPANY, ELKHART, INDIANA

pet. Do the valves move easily and quickly? Do the slides fit snugly, yet can they move in and out smoothly? Does the water-key spring keep it firmly against the instrument? The inspector corrects slight defects. All others are sent back to the production department.

Before the trumpet leaves the testing room, a performer plays the instrument, looking for any problems that the testing machines did not detect. The performer may be a trumpet player on the staff, or a professional musician who is hired to try out the instruments. If the instrument passes the expert's test for playing quality and pitch, it is given a final cleaning by hand. Then it is quickly sealed in a plastic bag to keep out all dust or dirt.

The wrapped instrument is either held in storage until it is ready to be shipped, or it is placed into a case and shipped out at once. Either way, sooner or later, it arrives for the professional player or student who has been waiting for this new trumpet.

4

The Trumpet Family

As a brass instrument, the trumpet is related to other members of the brass family: the French horn, trombone, and tuba. But it is part of an even more closely related family: trumpets of different sizes, the cornett and cornet, slide trumpet (described in Chapter 1), bugle and keyed bugle, demi-lune, and flugelhorn.

DIFFERENT-SIZED TRUMPETS

The most common trumpet is the one in B♭. When people say "trumpet," they usually mean the B♭ trumpet. This instrument became the standard sometime during the period when the natural trumpet was used with crooks of different lengths. Each crook changed the pitch of the trumpet as well as its tone quality.

In time, one crook became accepted over the others. Trum-

The most common trumpet is the B♭ trumpet.
PHOTOGRAPH ELEANOR BERGER

peters preferred this crook both for ease of playing and for beauty of tone. This particular crook put the trumpet in the key of B♭, leading to today's standard B♭ trumpet.

The trumpet is different from many other instruments in one respect. When a pianist, flutist, or violinist sees a C in the music, and plays a C, the instrument sounds a C. But when a trumpeter plays a C on a B♭ trumpet, the instrument sounds a B♭. In other words, the B♭ trumpet sounds one full step below the written note. This can be confusing. But so far, no

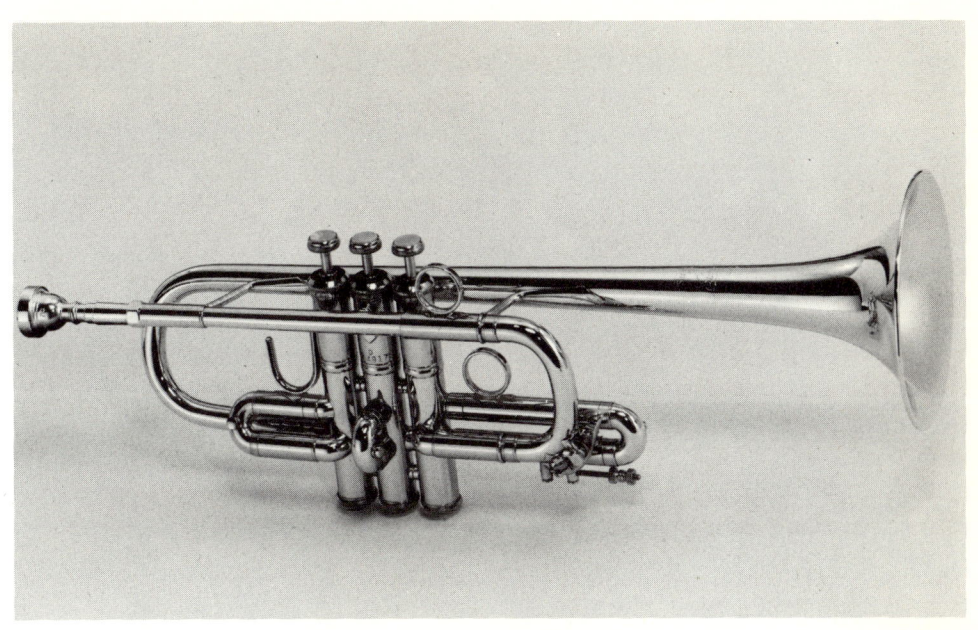

The D trumpet is smaller than the B♭ trumpet, and therefore plays higher.
COURTESY THE SELMER COMPANY, ELKHART, INDIANA

one has been willing to rewrite all the trumpet music to make the written notes and the sounding notes the same.

The C trumpet is slightly shorter than the B♭ trumpet, and is one tone higher in pitch. When the C trumpet plays a C, it sounds a C. Many trumpeters prefer the C over the B♭ trumpet for playing orchestra music. They find it has a more penetrating sound than the B♭, and blends in better with the other orchestra instruments.

When trumpeters play the music of Bach, Handel, or the other composers who wrote high clarino parts, they often use smaller trumpets keyed in D, E♭, F, G, or high A. Being smaller, they are higher in pitch, enabling the players to reach the clarino notes more easily.

The tiny piccolo B♭ trumpet
is half the length of the standard B♭ trumpet,
and therefore sounds an octave higher.
PHOTOGRAPH MELVIN BERGER

Mahillon, a firm of instrument makers in Brussels, Belgium, has created a special D trumpet to be used for playing Bach and Handel's clarino parts. It is 42 inches long, half the length of the natural trumpet in use in Bach and Handel's time. Therefore, it plays an octave, or eight notes, higher than the older instrument.

For very high parts, or for special effects, trumpeters sometimes use the piccolo trumpet. This tiny instrument is pitched in B♭, an octave above the standard B♭ trumpet. The tubing of the piccolo trumpet is half the length of the ordinary trumpet in B♭.

Most professional trumpeters have several different-sized trumpets so that they can choose the very best instrument for the music they are playing.

THE CORNETT

The cornett falls between the brass and woodwind families of instruments. Like the brass instruments, its sound is produced by the player's vibrating lips supported by a mouthpiece. Like the woodwind instruments, its pitch is changed by opening and closing holes along its length.

The cornett has a long and distinguished history. It dates back some 1500 years. The instrument was originally made from an animal horn. It received its name from the Italian word for horn, which is *corno*. Since it was usually made from a small horn, or *cornetto*, that is the name that stuck. In English it is called either cornett or cornetto.

This instrument is still being made and played today. Shepherds in remote areas of Norway and Sweden use cow and goat horns to make simple cornetts. They carve the narrow end of the horn into a mouthpiece. To change pitch, they drill several holes along the length of the horn.

They play their cornetts by buzzing their lips in the mouthpiece. To sound the lowest note, they cover all the holes with their fingers. This creates the longest vibrating column of air, and therefore the lowest note. To go higher, they uncover the holes one at a time, starting with the one farthest from the mouthpiece.

About 500 years ago, cornett makers began to construct the instrument of wood, instead of animal horn. From 1500 to 1650, wooden cornetts were among the most popular instruments. People heard them played together with trombones and the organ to accompany church choral music. The cornett

Copies of the cornett are still being made, and are used by trumpeters who specialize in playing old instruments.

also had a leading part in early orchestras and outdoor wind band concerts. And it was heard at big dinnertime concerts of the 16th century, and at large-scale entertainments. The cornett was admired for its soft tone, much like the human voice. Although it was a difficult instrument to blow, it could play fast, brilliant passages.

The mute cornett was slightly different from the cornett. It had a straight shape, instead of being curved, and the mouthpiece was carved out of the wood tubing of the instrument, instead of being separate. But it was played in the same way, and was similar in sound, although somewhat softer.

Toward the end of the 17th century, composers stopped writing parts for cornett. Other instruments were used to play their parts. They swiftly declined, and then disappeared altogether for about 250 years.

In our own time, there has been a rebirth of interest in the cornett. Modern makers are producing copies of the old instruments. Modern players are learning to play and perform on them.

The cornett today is made from a 24-inch length of a hard, close-grained wood, such as plum, pear, or maple. The wood is split in half lengthwise, and slightly conical channels are gouged out in each half. Both the channels and the wood are slightly curved.

The two halves are then glued tightly together. This creates a single channel which runs through the center of the wood. The outside is planed to create an eight-sided shape. It is covered with a thin piece of black leather. The leather is glued in place to prevent any air from leaking. Six holes are bored on the top to be covered with the fingers. One hole is bored in back to be covered by the thumb. The usual mouthpieces are made out of ivory, bone, or metal.

The cornett can be used to play all the notes in one octave. By blowing harder, the player can jump up and play all the notes of the scale one octave higher. These instruments can be heard in concerts of old music, when players try to recreate the sounds of the original instruments.

DEMI-LUNE

The demi-lune, or half-moon, trumpet was created in the early 18th century. It was part of an effort to improve the natural trumpet so that it could be played more in tune. This instrument was coiled. The player could push his hand in the bell, which lowered the pitch of any out-of-tune notes. The demi-lune, however, soon fell from favor, and exists today only in museums.

BUGLE

The first bugle was made from the horn of a young bull. It takes its name from the Old French word for young bull, *bugle*. The instrument was originally called a bugle-horn. In time, it was shortened to bugle.

In the Middle Ages, the bugle was used for hunting calls, for church ceremonies, and for military signals. Usually the instrument was worn on a shoulder sling and hung to the waist, so that it could quickly be lifted to the lips and sounded.

By the 17th century, the bugle still had the same horn shape, but was usually made of copper or brass. Now, in addition to its military uses, the bugle also was blown by town watchmen, and by drivers of the stagecoaches that carried the mail.

The bugle was given its present shape around the year 1800. Although they are not standardized in construction, most bugles are between 4 feet and 4½ feet in length. The tubing is doubled over two or four times.

The tubing is conical, ranging from a little less than ½ inch in diameter at the mouthpiece, to about 4 inches at the bell. Bugles used in England are more conical, and therefore sound more like the French horn. American bugles are less conical, and sound more like the trumpet.

The bugle can only play five notes. The only way that the player can change pitch is to tighten or to loosen the lips. This produces five notes of the overtone series. That is why bugle calls use no more than five notes. French bugle calls are even less varied. They use only four notes!

KEYED BUGLE

Kölbel, an instrument maker in St. Petersburg, Russia, found a way to increase the number of notes that could be played on the bugle. During the years from 1760 to 1770, he adapted a system of keys and holes similar to that used on woodwind instruments. The Kölbel instrument, called an *Amor Schall,* was quite popular for many years.

Near the bell of the bugle, Kölbel made two holes. He built flat, leather-covered keys to cover the holes. When the bugle player opened the hole closest to the bell, the vibrating length of the bugle was shortened a little bit. This raised the pitch of all the notes a half step. When the player opened both keys, the vibrating length was shortened some more. This raised all the notes a whole step.

Using the *Amor Schall* as a model, Anton Weidinger, a Viennese trumpet player, developed a keyed trumpet. It was so successful that Franz Joseph Haydn composed his trumpet concerto to be played on an early model.

The improved instrument had five keys, instead of two, and it used a more cylindrical tube, like the trumpet. This keyed instrument worked better than the *Amor Schall.* But Weidinger discovered that keys work better on a conical instrument like the bugle than they do on a cylindrical instrument like the trumpet.

In 1810, an Irish bandmaster named Joseph Halliday designed a keyed bugle, which he dedicated to the Duke of Kent.

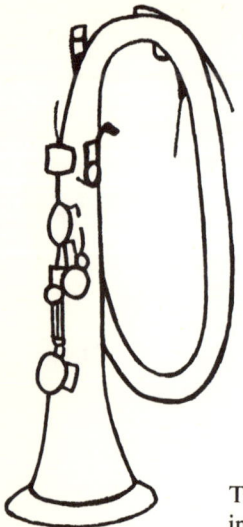

The holes covered by keys on this trumpet increased the number of notes that could be played.

It became known as the Kent bugle. This bugle had either five or six keys, and was able to play a complete scale. It became a popular brass solo instrument during the first half of the 19th century. Around 1850, though, it was replaced by the flugelhorn.

FLUGELHORN

The new valve for brass instruments was invented soon after the keyed bugle. No one knows the name of the instrument maker who had the idea of making a valved bugle to replace the keyed bugle. All that is known is that the first valved bugle was built in Vienna around the year 1830. It was named "flugelhorn," after the horn carried by the *flugelmeister*, an official at 18th century hunts in Germany.

The flugelhorn resembles a short, fat trumpet. It is about as long as the trumpet. It is, however, more conical and has more taper than the bugle. At the mouthpiece end, the tubing is about 7/16ths of an inch in diameter. It grows gradually wider

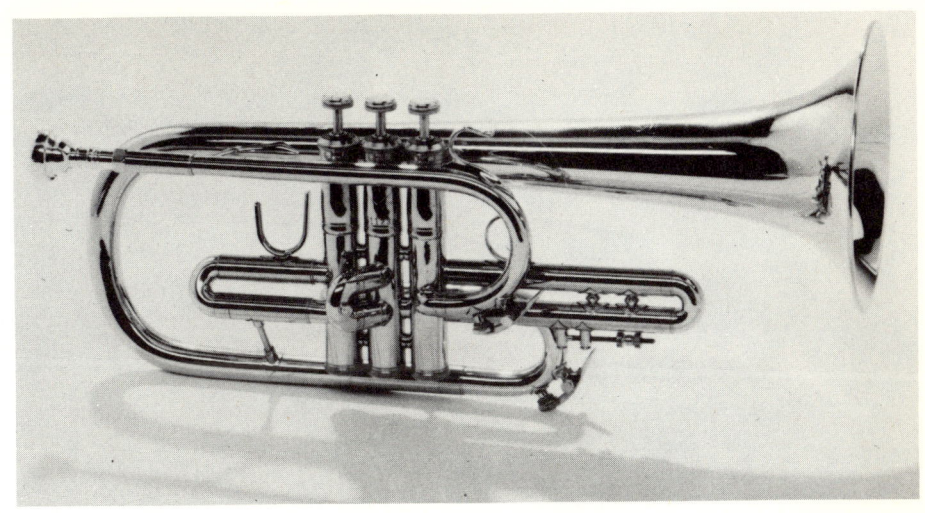

The flugelhorn is really a keyed bugle.
A number of modern jazz players
have revived this 19th century instrument.
COURTESY THE SELMER COMPANY, ELKHART, INDIANA

throughout the length of the tubing to a diameter of over 1 inch, before widening to a bell diameter of about 6 inches. The player rests his or her lips against a funnel-shaped mouthpiece. The instrument produces a dark, mellow tone.

The flugelhorn has maintained a modest position in the world of musical instruments. It is used in typical French or German military bands. The English include flugelhorns in their brass bands. And, occasionally, modern composers include parts for the flugelhorn. Ottorino Respighi wrote a passage for the flugelhorn in his 1924 orchestra composition, *Pines of Rome*. In that piece, the flugelhorn suggests the sound of the *buccina* carried by the armies of ancient Rome.

More recently, several leading jazz trumpeters have breathed new life into the old flugelhorn. Such well-known players as Chet Baker, Art Farmer, Shorty Rogers, and especially Miles Davis, began to use the flugelhorn in recordings and at per-

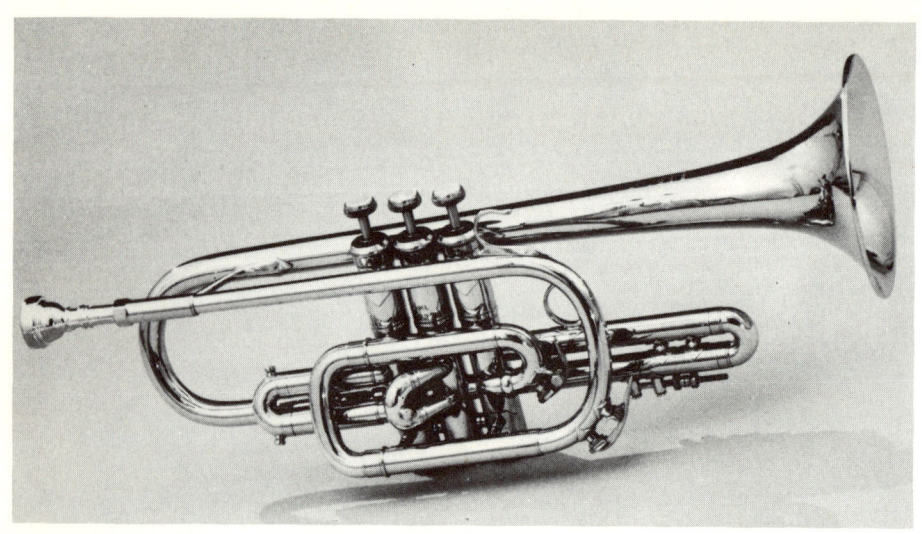

A close look at the cornet shows
that the tubing gradually grows wider
from the mouthpiece to the bell.
COURTESY THE SELMER COMPANY, ELKHART, INDIANA

formances. Today the smooth, rich, ample sound of the flugelhorn is a familiar part of modern jazz performances.

CORNET

While the flugelhorn was being created in Vienna, another instrument was being introduced in Paris. It was made by adding valves to a small, circular horn, known as the *cornet de poste*. The new instrument became known as the cornet.

Like the horn which preceded it, the cornet was basically conical in shape. At first, the cornet was played by horn players. But as the instrument began to be played with a mouthpiece similar to the trumpet mouthpiece, it was used by trumpet players.

During the 1830s, the cornet became one of the most popular instruments in Europe. It replaced the keyed bugle in popu-

The cornet is very similar to the trumpet. Here a cornet student (front) and trumpeter are playing together at a music lesson.
PHOTOGRAPH MELVIN BERGER

larity. The cornet player marched in military and brass bands. He played in theatres and in light opera orchestras. The most famous of the early cornet players was Jean Baptiste Arban (1825–1889), who taught at the Paris Conservatoire, conducted the orchestra at the Opera balls, and wrote several teaching methods for the cornet.

But the cornet never could shake its reputation for being a slightly vulgar instrument. It rarely found its way into the symphony orchestra. Its greatest use was as a solo instrument, frequently in works accompanied by a band. The most famous cornet soloist was the one with the Sousa Band, Herbert L. Clarke.

The largest relative of the trumpet is the bass trumpet. It is usually played by a trombonist.
PHOTOGRAPH MELVIN BERGER

Many jazz players prefer the seasoned sound of the cornet, which is closer to the sound of the human voice, than to the more brilliant sound of the trumpet. Louis Armstrong started his music studies on the cornet. Rex Stewart, Muggsy Spanier, Nat Adderley, and Thad Jones are important jazz cornet players of our day.

BASS TRUMPET

The bass trumpet is the largest member of the trumpet family.

It is about 8 feet long, or twice the length of the trumpet. Sometimes it has one more valve than the trumpet. This fourth valve lowers the pitch four tones.

The bass trumpet was suggested by the composer Richard Wagner in the middle of the 19th century. He wrote important parts for it in the four music dramas that make up his *Ring of the Nibelung*. Curiously enough, this distinctive instrument is usually played by a trombonist, rather than by a trumpet player, because of the size of the mouthpiece.

The B♭ trumpet is surely the leading member of the trumpet family. But the other instruments all have their place—for the special sounds they can create, and for playing music of the past.

5

Trumpet Players

Since the first trumpet player blew through a hollow tree branch long ago, countless people all over the world have played the trumpet and instruments that are closely related to the trumpet. Among these many players, a small number emerge as outstanding performers. In addition to their own unique skills, these players have many abilities in common. Their playing reveals a keen musical sense, with beauty of tone, fine expressive quality, and sensitivity for the particular style of the music. They are able to produce notes throughout the entire range, from top to bottom, accurately and cleanly. They have the technical ability to play fast, difficult passages at great speed. And they play in tune, with good rhythm.

Not too much is known about the outstanding players from the past. Those who are best remembered are known from their association with illustrious composers who wrote challenging parts for them.

PLAYERS FROM THE PAST

The English composer Henry Purcell wrote trumpet parts in his music for the player John Shore (1662-1752). From the important and difficult passages that appear in the scores, it is guessed that John Shore was an excellent performer. He is also credited with the invention of the tuning fork. In mid-career, he split his lip while playing the trumpet, and was not able to play again. Nevertheless, John Shore died a wealthy man, for he married a rich widow when he was 86 years of age.

While Purcell was writing for Shore, Johann Sebastian Bach was composing brilliant clarino parts for his leading trumpeter, Gottfried Reiche (1667-1734). A 1724 portrait by the artist Elias Haussmann shows Reiche holding a coiled circular trumpet. This painting furnishes scholars with evidence that Bach composed for this kind of trumpet.

Reiche gave the last performance of his life on October 5, 1734, at a concert for the Elector of Leipzig. The music included some very difficult trumpet parts that required great exertion. The performance was held in a large room lit by powerful torches. The next day, Reiche grew sick and died. The belief is that his death was caused by a combination of overexertion and and inhalation of the torches' poisonous fumes.

Two of the best-known trumpet concertos, those by Franz Joseph Haydn and Johann Nepomuk Hummel, were dedicated to Anton Weidinger (dates unknown), a trumpet player who lived in Vienna around the start of the 19th century. From the songlike slow sections and the brilliant fast sections of the two concertos, it is surmised that Weidinger was a very able performer on the *keyed trumpet*, which he helped to design in 1801.

MODERN TRUMPET PLAYERS

Very few names of the leading trumpet players of the 19th century are still remembered. At the very begininng of the 20th century, though, one player did rise to prominence—but he played the cornet, rather than the trumpet. Herbert L. Clarke (1867–1945) was the cornet soloist with the John Philip Sousa Band from 1904 to 1917.

During those years, and afterwards when he had his own band, Clarke was much admired both for the beauty of his tone and for the brilliance of his technique. A cornet solo by Clarke was always considered the high point of any band concert.

In addition to his fame as a performer, Clarke is also remembered as a composer. Many of the solo pieces he wrote for cornet or trumpet are still heard today, either in recitals or in solo appearances with band or orchestra.

We are fortunate to be living at a time when a good number of outstanding trumpet players are active. It is interesting to see how each one pursues different career goals.

Some very fine players are best known as orchestra musicians. These include Franz Kaderabek of the Philadelphia Orchestra, Adolph Herseth of the Chicago Symphony, Armando Ghitalla of the Boston Symphony, Thomas Stevens of the Los Angeles Philharmonic, and Bernard Adelstein of the Cleveland Orchestra. These players are also known as soloists and teachers.

The best-known trumpet soloist in the world today is the French performer, Maurice André. Upon graduation from the Paris Conservatoire, André was immediately appointed principal trumpet of the Orchestre National. But his amazing abilities soon launched him on a soloist's career. He has performed all over the world as an orchestra soloist, in recital, and on recordings. Other outstanding trumpet soloists include Martin Berinbaum of the United States, Edward Tarr of Switzerland, Adolf Scherbaum of Germany, and Timofey Dokschitser of the Soviet Union.

Maurice André, the best-known trumpet soloist in the world today, is shown here with several of the different-sized trumpets that he plays at his concerts.
COURTESY THE SELMER COMPANY, ELKHART, INDIANA

Robert Nagel, second from the right,
is an outstanding American trumpeter.
This photograph shows him with the other members
of the New York Brass Quintet,
a group that he helped organize.
COURTESY NEW YORK BRASS QUINTET

One of the most versatile players is the American trumpeter, Robert Nagel. A fine orchestra musician, soloist, chamber music player, and composer, Nagel is also a publisher of music for the trumpet and other brass instruments, as well as a very busy teacher.

Nagel started studying the trumpet at the age of 8 in the elementary school of his hometown, Freeland, Pennsylvania. After graduation from high school, he undertook further work in trumpet and musical composition at the Juilliard School of Music in New York City. His first job was in New York with the Little Orchestra Society. As a free-lance musician, he performed on radio and television, at ballets and operas, in recordings, and with numerous symphony orchestras.

In 1954, Nagel helped organize the New York Brass Quintet (two trumpets, French horn, trombone, and tuba). This group tours widely, giving between fifty and sixty concerts a year. They have recorded many excellent works written for brass quintet and other instrumental groups that include brass instruments. In his solo appearances, both in Europe and in America, Nagel performs various concertos, including his own Concerto for Trumpet and Orchestra.

Don Smithers's career as a trumpet player is quite different. He has become a leading performer and authority on trumpet music of the past. Smithers has devoted himself to the scholarly analysis of music, musicology, and to mastering the clarino and cornett music of bygone days.

Smithers's musical career started when he was a boy soprano in the Grace Church School choir in New York City. In high school, he sang tenor and began trumpet lessons. Around that time, he first heard a performance of Bach's *B Minor Mass*. Just hearing the thrilling clarino part led Smithers to a serious interest in the music of Bach, Handel, and other composers of the 18th century. After college, Don Smithers performed in the Bach *B Minor Mass* thirty-six times in a memorable nine-week tour of the Soviet Union.

Now Smithers holds a Ph.D. in musicology from Oxford University in England. In his musical research, he has uncovered

Don Smithers is a leading performer and authority on trumpet music of the past. Here he is shown with a special piccolo trumpet that he uses to play the high-pitched music from the period of Bach and Handel.

a number of little-known works for the trumpet. He has edited, performed, and recorded many of these compositions, some dating back over 300 years. Formerly on the faculty of Syracuse University in New York, he now teaches at the Royal Conservatory of Music at The Hague, Holland.

Carole Reinhart is a modern trumpet player who has a most interesting career. She is an outstanding performer and teacher. In addition, though, she works as a clinician for a leading trumpet manufacturer. She travels around the country to various schools, colleges, and conventions of music teachers giving lectures, demonstrations, master classes, and model lessons on the trumpet.

Carole Dawn Reinhart, shown in this photograph, is an outstanding player and teacher.
COURTESY GETZEN COMPANY, INC.

JAZZ TRUMPET PLAYERS

Everyone knows that New Orleans is the birthplace of jazz. But how many know *why* New Orleans has that distinction? The fact is that, after the Civil War, many discarded army band instruments ended up in New Orleans. By 1880, several Negro marching bands had been formed, using the cheap old army cornets, clarinets, trombones, and drums. These bands played at parades and funerals, and for other ceremonial occasions. Soon, players began to place accents on the weak beats of their marches. This practice gave rise to the characteristic beat of jazz.

The trumpet player who has been called "the greatest jazzman that ever lived," Louis Armstrong, was born in New Orleans on July 4, 1900. At an early age, he formed a singing group, The Singing Fools, with three friends. They sang on street corners, and passed around the hat for any pennies or nickels that they could get. While singing on New Year's Eve in 1913, an event occurred which changed the course of Louis' life.

To add to the excitement of the New Year's celebration, young Louis fired a shell from his father's pistol up into the air. A policeman, who happened by, arrested the boy. He was sentenced to $1\frac{1}{2}$ years in the Colored Waifs' Home for Boys.

In the Home, Louis received his first music instruction, at the outset on the drum, then the bugle, and finally on a beat-up old cornet. Before long, Louis Armstrong became leader of the band. He played a leading part on the cornet whenever the band played at outside parades, dances, or picnics. Because of his big, wide smile, the other boys at the Home nicknamed him Satchelmouth. Many years later, when he was touring England, his fans shortened it to a nickname that lasted all his life—Satchmo.

After leaving the Home, Satchmo did chores for the star cornet player in New Orleans, Joe "King" Oliver, in exchange for lessons. When Oliver left New Orleans for Chicago, in 1917, Louis took his seat in Kid Ory's Band, the most popular jazz group in New Orleans. At the age of 17, Louis "Satchmo" Armstrong became a professional musician.

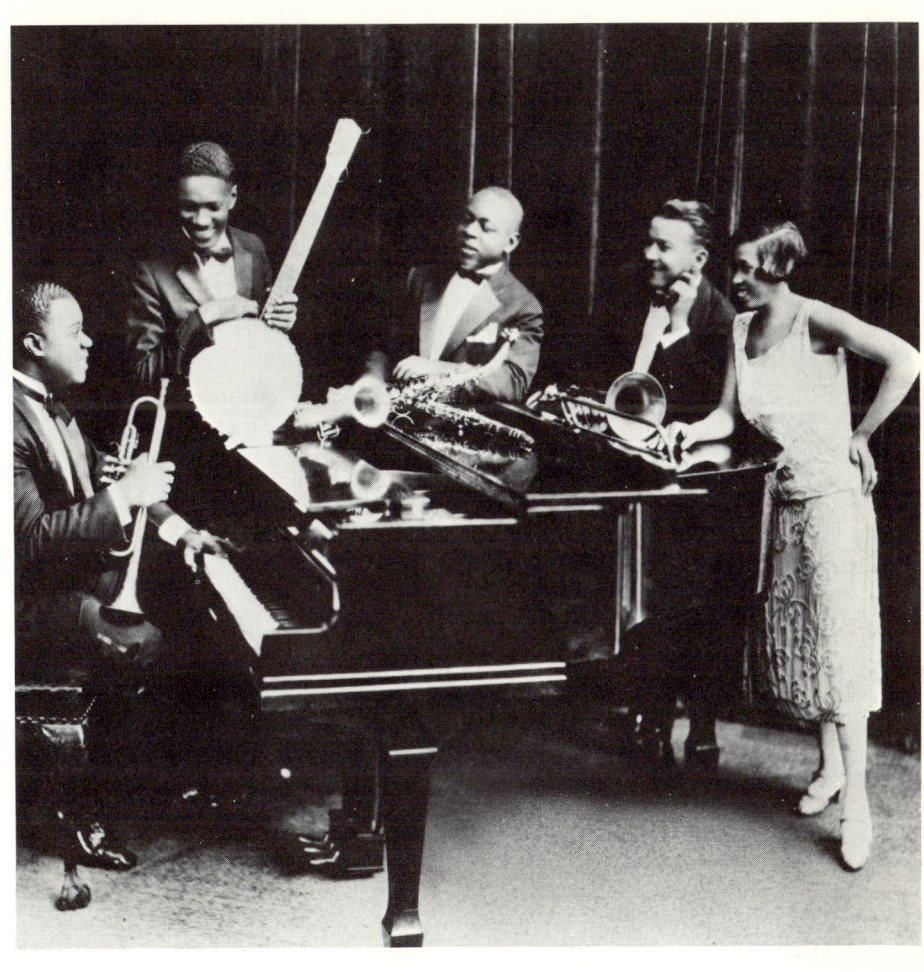

Louis Armstrong, seated at the piano, has been called "the greatest jazzman that ever lived."
COURTESY COLUMBIA RECORDS

Over the following years, Louis worked very hard at his music. "When I was a kid, I would rather do without food than without music," he once said. His career took him from New Orleans's riverboats, to King Oliver's band in Chicago, to New York in the Fletcher Henderson orchestra, and to a triumphal return to Chicago with his own band, Louis Armstrong and his Stompers.

Around the time Armstrong started his own band, he switched from cornet to trumpet. He also began the little habits that came to be identified with him: holding a big white handkerchief in his left hand as he grasped the trumpet; always greeting the audience with his growly voiced salute, "Oh yeah!" (He once said that, according to his mother, "Oh yeah" were the first words he ever uttered.)

The years with the Stompers were difficult years for Armstrong because he was having a great deal of trouble with his lips. Time after time, they would split and bleed. But Louis forced himself to keep on playing. He summed up his feeling by asking, "What's the good of having music in you, if you can't get it past your pucker?"

By 1948, the big band era was coming to a close. Louis formed a small group, the Louis Armstrong All Stars, made up of Louis, five other instrumentalists, and a vocalist. They toured all over the world, often representing the United States in foreign countries. His single biggest triumph, however, came with his 1963 recording of *Hello, Dolly*. It was so popular that there were times when it was broadcast around the country some ten thousand times a day. Louis performed it live very often, too. But each time he changed it a little, so that it would not become dull.

Starting in 1968, Louis' health began to fail. He was hospitalized several times. Finally on July 6, 1971, two days after his 71st birthday, Louis Armstrong died quietly at home in his sleep.

The only trumpet player who rivals Louis Armstrong as a legendary jazz great is Bix Beiderbecke (1903–1931). Bix was born Leon Bismark Beiderbecke to a white, middle-class family in Davenport, Iowa. His parents started him on piano lessons when he was a youngster, and he did very well. Later, he became interested in jazz. Just before his 16th birthday he borrowed a cornet from a friend and began teaching himself to play. A few months later, he bought his first instrument, a used cornet, for $35.

By the following year, he was playing in Neal Buckley's Novelty Orchestra at Linwood Park in Davenport and earning money as a musician. Many other groups followed, notably the Wolverines and the Jean Goldkette Orchestra, and Bix kept growing in ability and in fame. His warm tone, and subtle, gentle way of playing was winning him a widespread reputation.

But while he was scoring these triumphs on the trumpet, he was also drinking heavily and neglecting his health. Although he was still in his 20s, he was drunk, sick, and unhappy much of the time.

In October, 1927, Bix joined the well-known Paul Whiteman Orchestra. His drinking, which remained heavy, took an even greater toll. He frequently complained of feeling weak and tired. He missed rehearsals, and even some performances.

His decline accelerated until his death in 1931, at the age of 28. The death certificate listed the cause as pneumonia. But his friend, Frank Norris, came closer to the truth when he said, "He died of *everything*."

Dizzy Gillespie (born 1917) is a modern, trumpet-playing jazz giant. Born John Birks Gillespie, in Cheraw, South Carolina, Dizzy received his first music lessons on the trombone from his father, an amateur musician. One year later, he switched to trumpet.

In the 1940s, Dizzy, along with saxophonist Charlie Parker, began to develop a new style of playing jazz. It was a much more intellectual approach to music, with more complex mel-

This photograph of the Paul Whiteman Orchestra
was taken in 1928 when Bix Beiderbecke was a member.
Bix is standing third from the right in the rear row.
COURTESY THE WHITEMAN COLLECTION, WILLIAMS COLLEGE,
WILLIAMSTOWN, MASSACHUSETTS

odies and more advanced harmonies than what had come before. And Dizzy played in this new style with a speed and range that far surpassed most other trumpeters.

At first this new style was called "be-bop." Later it evolved into "modern" or "cool" jazz. It was the leading jazz style of the late 1940s and early 1950s.

Miles Davis (born 1926) played with the same style as Dizzy early in his professional career. But he went on to become even more cool, with a more delicate, muted tone. Sometimes he preferred to play the flugelhorn, with its rich, dark sound.

In the mid-1970s, Davis began combining the sounds of jazz and the more popular sounds of rock-'n'-roll. He uses electronic instruments, and sometimes even plays an amplified trumpet. In this way, he is introducing jazz to many young listeners who are only familiar with rock.

Miles Davis is one of the leading performers of the cool style of jazz trumpet playing.
COURTESY COLUMBIA RECORDS

With a powerful blast of air,
Maynard Ferguson reaches for one of
the very high notes for which he is famous.
COURTESY COLUMBIA RECORDS

Maynard Ferguson (born 1928) goes even further than Davis in accepting the style and sounds of rock. With his incredible high range, Ferguson and his band are very successful in attracting large audiences of young people.

Ferguson is also interested in helping young players. He conducts many teaching and demonstration clinics in schools all over the United States, and his native Canada. "I stress variety in my clinic work," Ferguson says. "I insist the listener and player get into all kinds of music. Don't get hung up on one idol. Love many musicians and styles. If I'm asked about players I like, I generally name at least fifty."

Harry James is well known, both as an outstanding jazz trumpeter and as the leader of his own big band.
COURTESY WILLARD ALEXANDER, INC.

Not only is Doc Severinsen well known for his trumpet playing, but he is also famous for his uncommon way of dressing.
COURTESY GETZEN COMPANY, INC.

A list of outstanding jazz trumpeters must surely also include names such as Nat Adderley, Chet Baker, Art Farmer, Harry James, Freddie Hubbard, Thad Jones, and Clark Terry. One of the most successful and popular of modern trumpeters is Carl "Doc" Severinsen (born 1927). Doc was originally called "Little Doc," since his father, a dentist and amateur violinist in Arlington, Oregon, was known as "Big Doc." It was Big Doc who started giving his son trumpet lessons when Little Doc was seven. Severinsen leads his band on a popular coast-to-coast television show. In addition, he appears in nightclubs and in concerts with his touring groups, The Now Generation Brass and Today's Children. He also performs as a soloist with symphony orchestras and concert bands.

Doc has some good advice for young musicians. He believes that they have the power and strength to accomplish almost anything they want—if they are willing to work for it. He says, "I often try to get junior high students to understand [that] if you just grab a hold of anything—your studies, your music—it can give you so much of a head start in life."

6

Trumpet Music

The trumpet is one of the most versatile of all musical instruments. One moment it can lead a full symphony orchestra to a climax of overwhelming strength and nobility. Another time it can growl out its own chorus in a small Dixieland combo. It can carry the singing melodic line in a trumpet concerto. It can also weave intricate patterns of sound in a brass quintet. It can startle with its power and brilliance, or it can charm with its warmth and humor. Its splendid, grand sounds can thrill thousands listening to a band at a parade or football game, while the quiet, mournful sound of the trumpet in a modern jazz group seems personal and intimate.

    The trumpet has all these different characters—and many more. For audiences to hear the trumpet's many moods, there must be players able to coax these varied sounds from their instruments. And there must be composers who know how to write for this instrument.

Music written for the trumpets of a marching band thrills thousands at a football game.
PHOTOGRAPH RUSS HAMILTON, COURTESY CORNELL UNIVERSITY

TRUMPETS IN THE ORCHESTRA

The earliest example of orchestra trumpet writing is found in the five-part fanfare at the opening of the Overture to the opera *Orfeo* by Claudio Monteverdi, composed in 1607. For the next 150 years, trumpet writing grew ever more difficult and demanding. This period marks the triumph of the clarino style, with its very high, light sound. It reached its climax in the music of Johann Sebastian Bach (*Brandenburg Concerto No. 2, B Minor Mass,* and several cantatas) and George Frideric Handel ("The Trumpet Shall Sound" from the *Messiah,* and his operas).

With the death of these two composers in the mid-18th century, and the falling away of clarino playing, the orchestra

Many trumpeters prefer to perform
old music on the original instruments.
PHOTOGRAPH HARRY POT

trumpet entered a period of decline. Inaccurate in pitch and unattractive in sound, it had a very limited appeal. Wolfgang Amadeus Mozart so disliked the trumpet of his day that he edited Handel's *Messiah,* and gave the high trumpet parts to the clarinet instead.

In the orchestra writing of Mozart, as well as that of Franz Joseph Haydn and Ludwig van Beethoven, the trumpet has a minor role to play. Usually the trumpet has long stretches of silence. When it enters, it serves mostly to add to the orchestral volume with loud sustained tones at the climax sections. An exception is Beethoven's *Third Leonore Overture,* where the trumpet is used for offstage fanfares. Beethoven included this part for the trumpet to suggest the approach of soldiers. The fanfare is played twice. The instructions in the music are that the trumpeter be closer to the stage for the second fanfare than for the first.

There is a well-known story connected with a performance of the *Third Leonore Overture* given some years ago at an outdoor concert in a park by the New York Philharmonic. About halfway through the *Overture,* the first trumpeter left his seat on the stage, and walked some distance away across a field to play the first fanfare.

Just as he was about to start, a policeman came running up to him. "You can't play here," the policeman said, grabbing for his trumpet. "Don't you see there's a concert going on?" It took some very fast and convincing explaining before the officer let him play the part.

The lowly position of the trumpet in the symphony orchestra lasted roughly 100 years—from about 1750 to 1850. Then, with the perfection of the valves for the trumpet, it returned to its old position of importance. Richard Wagner, in his operas and music dramas, wrote significant melodic parts for the trumpet. Other composers, such as Peter Ilyich Tchaikovsky, Richard Strauss, and Jean Sibelius, also gave the trumpet extended passages in their works for orchestra.

In the 20th century, the trumpet has achieved a leading role in many orchestra works. Among the compositions that feature the trumpet, there are *Quiet City* by Aaron Copland, *Petrushka* by Igor Stravinsky, Piano Concerto No. 1 by Dmitri Shostakovich, and William Walton's *Facade.*

The orchestral trumpet section
is kept busy when playing music
by composers who wrote in
the second half of the 19th century.
PHOTOGRAPH LOUIS HOOD,
COURTESY THE PHILADELPHIA ORCHESTRA

CONCERTOS FOR THE TRUMPET

Many trumpeters play in symphony orchestras. From time to time, they are asked to perform a concerto. A trumpet concerto is an extended work for solo trumpet accompanied by orchestra. Most are difficult to play. They give the solo performers a chance to show off the brilliance of their technique, the beauty of their tone, and the expressiveness of their interpretation of the music.

Concertos are usually divided into separate sections, called movements. There are usually pauses between the movements. A typical concerto has three movements: the first is moderately fast in speed, or tempo; the second is slow and songlike; and the third is very fast so the soloist can finish with a burst of dazzling speed. Altogether, a concerto takes about fifteen to twenty minutes to play.

Trumpet concertos can be divided into three groups. The concertos in the first group were composed in the period near the end of the 17th century, and during the early 18th century. This period in music is called the Baroque, and these works are referred to as Baroque trumpet concertos. The best-known of the Baroque trumpet concertos are those by George Frideric Handel, Georg Philipp Telemann, Tommaso Albinoni, Giuseppe Torelli, Heinrich von Biber, Johann Friedrich Fasch, and Johann Wilhelm Hertel.

The following period in music, the Classical period, lasted roughly from 1750 to 1800. There are five major trumpet concertos from the Classical period. The earliest is by Leopold Mozart, father of the famous Wolfgang Amadeus Mozart. The following concerto, by Franz Joseph Haydn, is the most popular of all trumpet concertos. There are more recordings of this concerto, a total of thirteen, than of any other trumpet concerto.

Michael Haydn, brother of Franz Joseph, wrote two concertos that are performed, and have been recorded. But neither ever reached the popularity of Franz Joseph's work. The final Classical concerto is the one by Johann Nepomuk Hummel, a leading Viennese composer.

Both the Joseph Haydn and the Hummel concertos were written for the keyed trumpet. They were dedicated to Anton Weidinger, an outstanding performer of the time, and the man who had helped to develop the keyed trumpet. Today, though, both concertos are played on the standard valved trumpet.

During the 19th century, which is the Romantic period, almost no trumpet concertos were written that are still remembered and performed today.

The 20th century is the modern period of trumpet composition. Among the well-known modern concertos are those by Henri Tomasi, André Jolivet, Karl Pilss, and Robert Nagel. The great trumpet teacher, Ernest Williams, wrote a series of six trumpet concertos. And three recent trumpet concertos from the Soviet Union are sometimes played. They are by Alexander Arutunian, Vladimir Kriukov, and Moysey Vainberg.

SONATAS FOR THE TRUMPET

When trumpet players give recitals they are usually accompanied by piano. One musical form that is frequently heard at recitals is the sonata. A sonata is similar to a concerto, except that the trumpet is accompanied by piano, instead of by orchestra.

There are just two main groups of trumpet sonatas. The first group dates from the Baroque period. It includes sonatas by Arcangelo Corelli, Giuseppe Torelli, Domenico Gabrieli, Heinrich von Biber, Johann Heinrich Schmelzer, Domenico Alberti, and Giuseppe Maria Iacchini.

The next group of trumpet sonatas comes from the 20th century. The outstanding sonatas from this period are those by Paul Hindemith, Halsey Stevens, and Kent Kennan. Jean Françaix and Walter Hartley wrote sonatinas, slightly shorter works than sonatas.

OTHER TRUMPET SOLOS AND CHAMBER MUSIC

Besides the concertos and sonatas, there are many other solo works for trumpet. There are marches, fanfares, rondos, suites, sinfonias, minuets, dances, variations, fantasies, and pieces with many other titles. Some of these are easy pieces, composed mostly as student works, to help young performers master the trumpet. Others are quite difficult, and are written with the advanced or professional performer in mind.

In addition to these trumpet works, there are a vast number of cornet solos, mostly to be played with piano accompaniments. Herbert L. Clarke is perhaps the most popular composer of cornet solos. Among his better known works are *From the Shores of the Mighty Pacific, The Southern Cross, Bride of the Waves, Stars in the Velvety Sky,* and *Sounds from the Hudson.*

The trumpet is also used in various chamber music combinations. These range from works for two, three, or four trumpets, to full brass ensembles. One of the most popular chamber music groups is the brass quintet, which consists of two trumpets, French horn, trombone and tuba.

It is very difficult to list the outstanding jazz or popular music for trumpet. Jazz trumpeters almost always improvise when they play. They learn the melody by ear, and then make up their own variations on the melody as they go along. When a pop group does play from printed music, the members use special arrangements that are seldom published or for sale.

Also, many of the melodies of jazz and pop music were originally songs, written to be sung with words. They would have

A trumpet soloist, such as Martin Berinbaum, owns a collection of different types of trumpets. Can you recognize the natural trumpet and the circular trumpet?
PHOTOGRAPH SHELDON SOFFER

Jazz trumpeters, like Maynard Ferguson, either play special arrangements or they improvise.
COURTESY G. LEBLANC CORPORATION

to be arranged to be playable on trumpet. Many pop hits are famous for a while, and then are quickly forgotten, so that there rarely are printed editions.

In any case, between the orchestra music, concertos, sonatas and other solo works, and chamber music, there is a vast amount of music for trumpet, to be played alone or with others. And the list is growing all the time. Composers write new compositions. Scholars discover old music. Arrangers prepare music written for other instruments to be played on the trumpet. There is something in this great variety of music to suit every taste.

7

You and the Trumpet

The exciting sounds of the trumpet are easily available to everyone. You can hear trumpets at concerts of symphony orchestras, pop groups, and concert bands. You can also hear trumpets at recitals by trumpet soloists and in small groups that include the trumpet. To find out about these events, you should read the concert announcements in the newspaper. Perhaps you can place your name on the mailing lists of any local concert-giving organizations—symphony, band, college, high school, music school, art center, museum, church—so they will let you know about upcoming concerts and recitals.

In addition, you can hear trumpets in the theater, when there is a pit orchestra playing for a musical show, an opera, or a ballet. And you can always hear trumpets on records, radio, and television.

What should you listen for when you hear a trumpet performance?

First and foremost, you should listen for the overall musical effect. Listen for the design or pattern of the music. Try to sense the mood or character the composer is trying to convey.

Then focus your attention on the trumpet or trumpets. Are they being used as melody instruments or just to fill in the loud sections? (Can you relate this to what you now know about the historical development of the trumpet?) Do the trumpets play mostly by themselves or with the other brass instruments? Do they blend in well? How does the trumpet part fit in with the other instruments of the band, orchestra, or group?

Finally, listen to the quality of the trumpet playing. How is the tone? Does the player change the tone quality for different pieces? Does the player hide his or her breathing, or does it interrupt the flow of the music? Is the playing expressive of the feelings the composer put into the work? If it is jazz, does the trumpeter play interesting and original improvisations? Is the trumpet in tune? Are there any mistakes, any missed notes?

Perhaps the best advice, though, is to attend performances including the trumpet as often as possible. The more you hear, the more you will enjoy and appreciate this noble instrument.

One of the results of listening to the trumpet is that you may decide to learn how to play the trumpet. The chance to learn to play the trumpet is also open to all. At one time, just boys played the trumpet. But for some time now, girls have been playing the trumpet in increasing numbers. There may be a few cases where irregular teeth, unusually shaped lips, or a disease that prevents easy and deep breathing *might* interfere with playing the trumpet. But these problems can usually be overcome. If you have any questions, ask a trumpet teacher for advice.

Every year, many thousands of students begin their studies on the trumpet. Perhaps you are one of those who are about to start lessons. Here is what you can expect.

Some beginning students rent a used trumpet at first. It costs little, and it gives you a chance to decide if you are fitted for the trumpet and if the trumpet is the best instrument for you.

Other students decide to buy a trumpet right at the outset. New trumpets range in price from about $150 for a good student model to about $600 for a fine professional instrument. Used instruments can, of course, be bought at much lower prices.

In buying an instrument, it is good to be able to consult with your teacher. He or she will check that the valves work easily and well, and that there is no serious damage to the metal of the instrument. Your teacher will also suggest the exact mouthpiece that is best suited to your lips and your teeth.

Most trumpet students start their lessons in school. Often elementary schools offer group lessons in each of the instruments around fourth grade. Some students, however, study with a private teacher outside of the school. Here the teacher only works with one student at a time, either in the teacher's studio, in the student's home, or at a music school.

No matter where you study, the first few lessons are about the same. First, most teachers show you how to set your lips in the right position, called an **embouchure.** They instruct you in the way to place the mouthpiece in the center of your lips. Then they help you buzz with your lips into the mouthpiece.

From the first lesson on, teachers usually stress **tonguing.** This involves using the tongue to attack each note sharply and cleanly. The correct way to tongue the trumpet is to place the tip of the tongue between the front teeth. Then, when you begin the note, you pull your tongue sharply back, as though you were going to say "too." Tonguing is used to start notes; it is never used to end a note.

Many trumpet students begin with group lessons in school.
PHOTOGRAPH MELVIN BERGER

Teachers also help you focus your attention on the correct way to breathe. Although you have been breathing since you were born, you probably have not been breathing in the most efficient way for playing the trumpet. Trumpet teachers explain the importance of your diaphragm, the large sheet of muscle that separates your chest from your abdomen. When you lower your diaphragm and move your ribs up and out, air rushes into your lungs. Then, when you raise your diaphragm, it forces the air out.

Young trumpet players are usually surprised to learn that you do not breathe in through your nose when you play the trumpet. Even though the mouthpiece is holding the center of your lips together, you learn to take in a great deal of air quickly through the corners of your mouth. You then exhale it slowly

107

The trumpet teacher points to the new lesson in the method book. The student will practice it at home, and play it for her teacher next week.
PHOTOGRAPH MELVIN BERGER

through the instrument to produce the sound. Since breathing is so basic to playing the trumpet, most players do not smoke, since smoking cuts the capacity of the lungs to hold air.

Once you have begun to understand buzzing into the mouthpiece, embouchure, tonguing, and breathing, you are ready to produce a sound on your trumpet. The teachers show you how to insert the mouthpiece into the trumpet, and how to buzz into the instrument. They also show you how to hold the trumpet, grasping the instrument with your left hand, and placing the fingertips of your right hand on the tops of the valves.

Most lessons involve the use of a method or lesson book. The book consists of exercises and pieces that teach you to read music and to develop trumpet-playing technique, by going from easy to increasingly more difficult music.

At each lesson, teachers introduce students to something new —a new note, a new rhythm, a more difficult pattern. They explain it, play it for you, and give you a chance to try it. Then, since most lessons are once a week, you take the book home and practice what you have learned. The secret of success in learning how to play the trumpet is home practice. Daily, careful practice at home, from one half hour a day for beginners up to several hours a day for advanced students, is a guarantee of success. Then, at the end of the week, when you return for your next lesson, the teacher listens to the material you practiced. Necessary corrections or suggestions are made. And then it is on to some new music for the following week.

It takes several years, and many, many hours of practice to master the trumpet. But if you ask any trumpet player, he or she will tell you that the pleasures, satisfactions, and rewards of playing make it all worthwhile.

CARING FOR THE TRUMPET

As one trumpet player said, "A trumpet should last forever as long as you keep it clean—and don't sit on it!" Just about the only part of the trumpet that ever wears out is the cork on the water key!

Teachers usually instruct their students in how to care for their instruments. The first rule is to keep the trumpet in its case whenever it is not in use. This prevents any bangs or dents that harm the sound and the appearance of the instrument.

One important rule of caring for the trumpet is to remove the mouthpiece when not playing.
PHOTOGRAPH ELEANOR BERGER

Another rule is always to remove the mouthpiece after playing. This helps avoid a major problem—a stuck mouthpiece. More damage is caused by students trying to remove a stuck mouthpiece by force than any other single cause. If you cannot easily remove the mouthpiece by hand, use the mouthpiece puller that is especially designed for that purpose. (Most teachers have one.) If the puller does not do the trick, take the trumpet to a repair shop. It may save you more costly repair bills later on.

About once a month, you should clean the trumpet by running water through the entire instrument. As the water flows through the tubing, move the valves up and down, to send water through the valve chambers and slides as well. From time to time, add some mild detergent to the water for a more thorough cleaning.

The mouthpiece, too, should be cleaned monthly. Use a wooden toothpick to remove any bits of dirt. Then use water, or soap and water, to flush it clean.

The usual cause of sluggish valves is dirt in the valve casings. Use soap and water to clean them out several times a year. Always keep them greased with a few drops of valve oil. Before adding the oil, though, remove the old oil with a soft clean cloth. Handle the valves very carefully when you remove them, and make sure you replace them in the proper casings.

Most trumpets have a lacquer finish, which will be damaged or destroyed by metal polish, or a strong soap or cleaner. Use only a soft cloth, wet or dry, to clean the instrument, and a lacquer polish to add lustre.

PERFORMANCE

Soon after you begin your trumpet studies, you may join a school band or orchestra. In these groups you will play music especially composed for school use. These pieces are fun to play, and they also help you master your instrument. Most elementary bands and orchestras present a few concerts a year for parents and other students. As you go on to junior and senior high, you will play music by famous composers and appear in more concerts every year.

You may also play in a variety of different musical groups. There may be a marching band that plays at football and perhaps basketball games, and marches in community parades.

Young trumpet players
usually give their first performances
as members of a school band or orchestra.
PHOTOGRAPH MELVIN BERGER

Usually the marching band members wear very attractive uniforms when they perform. In addition, many schools also have a pop-music group, called a stage band, dance band, jazz band, or similar name.

Some schools even offer additional playing opportunities. They may have a brass quintet, or they may be able to place the trumpet player in a small group of two, three, or four trumpets. Besides these groups, you may have a chance to play a solo at a school concert.

TRUMPET PLAYING AS A PROFESSION

Most boys and girls study the trumpet just for the fun of it. As

The trumpeters in the high school band
wear attractive uniforms at their concerts.
PHOTOGRAPH ELEANOR BERGER

they go along, they may find that they enjoy the instrument very much. Often, those who like it the most have a talent for the instrument, learn quickly, and play very well. A number of these players decide to make trumpet playing their career. They set out to become professional musicians.

Some students who started playing in elementary school become professional players on graduation from high school. Although a college degree is not required to become a professional musician, a large percentage of players do go to college. Many attend conservatories, which are colleges devoted to the teaching of music. Here they are able to spend most of their time on their instruments and music studies, with few added required courses. Others attend regular colleges where they major in

In addition to bands and orchestras, trumpet players may also play in school brass quintets.
PHOTOGRAPH MELVIN BERGER

music, but take a number of other courses as well. A good performer has an excellent chance of winning a scholarship to a college or conservatory, and also has a way to earn some extra money performing for various functions.

After graduation, many trumpet players find positions in the one hundred and twenty professional symphony orchestras in the United States. A full-sized orchestra has four trumpet players; smaller ones have two or three. A typical orchestra has four or five rehearsals, and two or more concerts every week, for a season lasting about forty weeks. Every large city in the country has its own orchestra.

Professional trumpet players frequently perform in the pit for musical shows, operas, and ballet. The next time you are

Some trumpet players play in college marching bands.
PHOTOGRAPH RUSS HAMILTON, COURTESY CORNELL UNIVERSITY

in a theater with a pit orchestra, look in front of the stage for the trumpet players. Also look for trumpet players in professional concert bands that are active in the summer, giving outdoor concerts in many cities and towns around the country.

There are probably more professional trumpet players in the pop music field than anywhere else. They play for recordings of jazz groups and pop singers, for TV and radio, for commercials, in theaters and nightclubs, at weddings and other parties, and in movie studios.

Musicians often increase their income from playing by giving private lessons. If they wish to teach trumpet in the public schools, they must earn a college degree in music education. Usually a school music teacher is able to play and teach several instruments, as well as conduct a band or an orchestra.

Almost every professional trumpet player does some amount

Many professional trumpet players
find positions in symphony orchestras.
This is the view from the trumpet section.
COURTESY COLUMBIA ARTISTS MANAGEMENT

of private teaching, on a part-time basis. They devote a few hours a week to teaching, and spend the rest of their time practicing, rehearsing, and performing.

Most musicians enjoy teaching. They like to see students improve under their guidance. They take delight in passing on the traditions of trumpet playing that they acquired from their teachers. And they all can use the added income that teaching provides.

People who enjoy playing the trumpet very much, and are successful, but still do not want to make it their life work, can continue to play the trumpet as a hobby. They become amateur musicians. Almost every town or city in the country has its own

One of the most famous theater orchestras
is in New York City's Radio City Music Hall.
Do you see the trumpets
just in front of the drums on the right?
PHOTOGRAPH IMPACT, COURTESY RADIO CITY MUSIC HALL

England's Grimelthorpe Colliery Band is an amateur group of coal miners. This outstanding band has made several recordings and television appearances and has toured the United States.
PHOTOGRAPH SOPHIE BAKER, COURTESY GRIMELTHORPE COLLIERY BAND

amateur orchestra or band. Many colleges also have groups that are open to everyone.

These groups usually rehearse one evening a week. This makes it possible for people who are busy with other jobs all day to play. Most of these groups give a few concerts each year.

Trumpet players who are interested in keeping up with the latest news concerning the trumpet can join the International Trumpet Guild. This fine organization publishes both a Newsletter and a Journal filled with material on trumpet performances, teaching, and literature. For information, write to David Baldwin, Secretary, International Trumpet Guild, 589 Lincoln Avenue, St. Paul, Minnesota 55102.

Listener or player, beginner or advanced, professional or amateur, you will find the trumpet one of the most attractive and fascinating of all musical instruments.

Glossary

ANTI-NODE: The point, in a sound wave, of greatest vibration.

B♭ TRUMPET: The leading member of the trumpet family; usually just called trumpet.

BASS TRUMPET: The lowest-pitched relative of the trumpet. Suggested by the composer Richard Wagner, in the mid-19th century.

BELL: The wide flared opening of the trumpet that helps to project the sound.

BRASS: A mixture of the metals copper (about 70%) and zinc (about 30%).

BRASS QUINTET: The most popular brass chamber music group, consisting of two trumpets, French horn, trombone and tuba. Also music for this combination.

BUGLE: A brass-wind instrument similar to the trumpet, but with more conical tubing, and without valves.

BUSINE: The longest trumpet of the Middle Ages.

CAPISTRUM: A head and face band worn by trumpeters in ancient Rome.

CLARINO: A style of high, brilliant trumpet playing that reached its peak in the 18th century.

CONCERTO: A composition, usually in three separate movements, for a solo instrument accompanied by orchestra.

CORNET: A wind instrument very similar to the trumpet, the main difference being that the cornet has a slightly more conical tube.

CORNETT: An instrument that produces its sound by the player's vibrating lips, but that changes pitch by opening and closing holes along the length of the instrument.

CROOK: A length of tubing inserted into the trumpet tubing to raise or lower the pitch of the instrument.

DEMI-LUNE: A type of natural trumpet that was circular in shape, so the player could lower the pitch by inserting his hand in the bell. Also called half-moon.

DIDJERIDOO: A very ancient type of trumpet, still being played by some primitive tribes in Australia.

EMBOUCHURE: Formation of the lips and mouth for playing a wind instrument such as the trumpet.

FLUGELHORN: A bugle with valves.

FUNDAMENTAL NOTE: A note produced when a musical instrument is vibrating as a whole, and not in parts.

HATZOTZEROTH: An ancient trumpet described in the Bible.

KEYED BUGLE: A bugle with holes in the tubing that were opened and closed with keys, increasing the number of notes that could be played.

KEYED TRUMPET: A trumpet with holes in the tubing that were opened and closed with keys, increasing the number of notes.

LACQUER: A type of varnish made of shellac dissolved in alcohol. Used on the brass of the trumpet.

LITUUS: A J-shaped ancient Roman trumpet, played by mounted soldiers.

MOUTHPIECE: A separate section inserted into the tubing to support the player's vibrating lips.

MUTE: A separate device placed in the trumpet bell to change or soften the trumpet tone.

NATURAL TRUMPET: The major type of trumpet that was popular in the years from about 1500 to 1800.

NODE: The point, in a sound wave, of no vibration.

OCTAVE: The distance between two notes, eight notes apart, that have the same letter name.

OVERTONES: The series of notes produced by multiplying the vibrating speed of the fundamental note by two, three, four, five, or a higher whole number.

PITCH: How high or low a note sounds. It depends on the speed of vibration—the faster the vibrations, the higher the pitch.

PRINCIPALE: The lowest part of the range of the natural trumpet.

SALPINX: The ancient Greek trumpet, about 5 feet long.

SHOFAR: An ancestor of the trumpet, made from an animal horn. Still used in Jewish religious ceremonies.

SLIDE TRUMPET: A trumpet used from the 15th through the 19th centuries. The player changed pitch by sliding the trumpet itself up or down the length of the mouthpiece neck.

SONATA: A composition, usually in three separate movements, for one or two instruments. Trumpet sonatas are for trumpet and piano.

SOUND: Anything that can be heard; produced by rapid vibration.

STADTPFEIFER: Town trumpeters who played for feasts, celebrations, and other state occasions.

THURMER: Tower trumpeters who stood watch from a church tower or other high point, and sounded warnings with their trumpets.

TONE COLOR: The quality of sound produced by a musical instrument.

TONGUING: The use of the tongue to interrupt the flow of air, giving each note a clean, sharp start.

TROMBA: The Italian word for trumpet; also refers to one part of the range of the natural trumpet.

TRUMPET: A brass-wind instrument. Highest-pitched member of the brass-wind family.

TUBA: A straight-tubed ancient Roman trumpet, played by marching soldiers. Also a modern low-pitched brass instrument.

TUNING SLIDE: A U-shaped length of tubing that can be pulled out or pushed in to raise or lower the pitch of the trumpet.

VALVE: A device that enables the player easily and quickly to increase the length of the vibrating air column of the trumpet.

VIBRATION: A rapid shaking back and forth. All sound is vibration.

The Trumpet on Records

The following list of recordings is organized according to the trumpet soloist. New recordings are always being made, and old recordings go out of print. Good sources for up-to-date information on recordings are put out by:

>W. Schwann, Inc.
>137 Newbury Street
>Boston, Mass. 02116

The *Schwann Record and Tape Guide* is published monthly, and lists all current recordings, organized by composers. The *Schwann Artist Issue* is published from time to time, and lists the available recordings, organized by performers.

PERFORMER	COMPOSER/TITLE	RECORDING COMPANY
André, Maurice	Fasch: Concerto	Deutsche Grammophon
André, Maurice	Haydn: Concerto M. Haydn: Concerto in D Richter: Concerto	Deutsche Grammophon
André, Maurice	Haydn: Concerto Albinoni: Concerto Hummel: Concerto Telemann: Concerto Torelli: Concerto Vivaldi: Concerto	RCA

123

PERFORMER	COMPOSER/TITLE	RECORDING COMPANY
André, Maurice	Hummel: Concerto L. Mozart: Concerto Telemann: Concerto Vivaldi: Concerto	Angel
André, Maurice	Jolivet: Concerto	Westminster
Berinbaum, Martin	Haydn: Concerto Hummel: Concerto Torelli: Sinfonie Albinoni: Sonata	Vanguard
Blee, Eugene	Nagel: Concerto	CRI
Darling, James	Stevens: Sonata Kennan: Sonata	Advent
Delmotte, Roger	Purcell: Sonata	Nonesuch
Dokschitser, Timofey	Arutunian: Concerto Kriukov: Concerto Vainberg: Concerto	Melodiya/Angel
Ghitalla, Armando	Albrechtsberger: Concerto Molter: Concerto Hummel: Concerto	Cambridge
Ghitalla, Armando	Copland: *Quiet City* M. Haydn: Concerto Selig: *Mirage*	Cambridge
Nagel, Robert	Bach: *Brandenburg Concerto No. 2*	Columbia
New York Brass Quintet	*In Concert*	Golden Crest

PERFORMER	COMPOSER/TITLE	RECORDING COMPANY
Scherbaum, Adolf	Bach: *Brandenburg Concerto No. 2*	Angel
Schwarz, Gerard	Albinoni: Concerto Hertel: Concerto Telemann: Concerto	Desto
Smithers, Don	*Baroque Trumpet Anthology*	Philips
Smithers, Don	*Baroque Trumpet Concertos*	Philips
Smithers, Don	*Music for Trumpet and Cornetto*	Argo
Stevens, Thomas	Hindemith: Sonata Stevens: Sonata	GSC
Tarr, Edward	Hertel: Concerto Hummel: Concerto L. Mozart: Concerto	Nonesuch
Thibaud, Pierre	Hummel: Concerto Jolivet: Concertino Telemann: Concerto Tomasi: Concerto	Deutsche Grammophon
Vacchiano, William	Shostakovich: Piano Concerto No. 1	Columbia
Wilbraham, John	Biber: Sonatas	Nonesuch

JAZZ AND POPULAR TRUMPET PLAYERS

PERFORMER	COMPOSER/TITLE	RECORDING COMPANY
Adderley, Nat	*Scavenger*	Milestone
Baker, Chet	*She Was Too Good to Me*	CTI
Armstrong, Louis	*Hello, Dolly*	MCA
Armstrong, Louis	*At the Crescendo*	MCA
Beiderbecke, Bix	*The Bix Beiderbecke Story*	Columbia
Davis, Miles	*Basic Miles*	Columbia
Davis, Miles	*Live-Evil*	Columbia
Farmer, Art	*Farmer's Market*	Prestige
Ferguson, Maynard	*Chameleon*	Columbia
Ferguson, Maynard	*M.F. Horn Two*	Columbia
Gillespie, Dizzy	*My Way*	Solid State
Hubbard, Freddie	*First Light*	CTI
Jones, Thad	*Thad Jones/Mel Lewis*	Blue Note
Severinsen, Doc	*Brass Roots*	RCA
Stewart, Rex	*Memorial Album*	Prestige

Index

André, Maurice, 78
Arban, Jean Baptiste, 73
Armstrong, Louis, 74, 84-86

B♭ trumpet, 61-62, 63, 75
Bach, Johann Sebastian, 25, 26, 63, 64, 77, 81, 95
Bach trumpets, 25
bands, 111, 112, 118
bass trumpet, 74-75
Beiderbecke, Bix (Leon Bismark), 86-87
bell, 44-49
Blühmel, Friedrich, 29
brass, 42-44
buccina, 23, 71
bugle, 35, 68-69
buzz mute, 41

C trumpet, 25, 63

clarino, 25-26, 28, 63, 81, 95
Clarke, Herbert L., 73, 78, 101
cornet, 72-74, 84
cornett, 65-67
crook, 28-29, 61-62
cup mute, 39

D trumpet, 25, 63, 64
Davis, Miles, 71, 88, 90
demi-lune trumpet, 68
derby mute, 40-41
didjeridoo, 15

Egyptian trumpets, 16, 17
embouchure, 106

Ferguson, Maynard, 90
flugelhorn, 70-72, 88

Gillespie, Dizzy (John Birks), 87-88

Handel, George Frideric, 25, 63, 64, 81, 99
Harmon mute, 40
hatzotzeroth, 16-19
Haydn, Franz Joseph, 69, 77, 96, 99-100

International Trumpet Guild, 118

Kent bugle, 69-70
keyed bugle, 69, 70, 72
keyed trumpet, 69, 77

lessons, 106-109
lituus, 20

mouthpiece, 11, 25, 26, 106, 107, 108, 110, 111
mute cornett, 67
mutes, 39-41

Nagel, Robert, 80-81, 100
natural trumpet, 24-26, 28

orchestras, 11, 114, 118
overtones, 34, 35, 69

piccolo trumpet, 25, 64
plunger mute, 41

Reiche, Gottfried, 77

Reinhart, Carole, 82
Roman trumpet, 19-20

salpinx, 19
Severinsen, Doc (Carl), 92-93
shofar, 16
slide trumpet, 26-28
Smithers, Don, 81-82
sound waves, 33, 34, 35
Stölzel, Heinrich, 29
straight mute, 39

tonguing, 106
tromba da tirarsi, 26
trompette des menéstrel, 26
trumpet
   concertos, 77, 99-100
   family, 13, 61-75
   players, 16, 19, 20, 23-24, 65, 76-93
   sonatas, 100-101
tuba, Roman, 19-20
tuning slide, 38-39

valves, 35-37, 53-54
   care of, 111
   invention of, 29-30

water key, 39, 109
"Wa-Wah" mute, 40
Weidinger, Anton, 69, 77, 100